YA
26.95

OCT   2005

ARBITRARY BORDERS

Political Boundaries in World History

ARBITRARY BORDERS

Political Boundaries in World History

The Great Wall of China

Louise Chipley Slavicek

Foreword by
Senator George J. Mitchell

Introduction by
James I. Matray
California State University, Chico

CHELSEA HOUSE
P U B L I S H E R S
A Haights Cross Communications Company

Philadelphia

For Debra J. Kraft
• • •

FRONTIS This map shows the Great Wall and a few of its branches.

CHELSEA HOUSE PUBLISHERS

VP, NEW PRODUCT DEVELOPMENT Sally Cheney
DIRECTOR OF PRODUCTION Kim Shinners
CREATIVE MANAGER Takeshi Takahashi
MANUFACTURING MANAGER Diann Grasse

Staff for THE GREAT WALL OF CHINA

EXECUTIVE EDITOR Lee Marcott
PRODUCTION EDITOR Noelle Nardone
SERIES AND COVER DESIGNER Keith Trego
PHOTO EDITOR Sarah Bloom
LAYOUT EJB Publishing Services

A Haights Cross Communications ◥ Company

www.chelseahouse.com

First Printing

9 8 7 6 5 4 3 2 1

Library of Congress Cataloging-in-Publication Data
Slavicek, Louise Chipley, 1956–
  The great wall of China / Louise Chipley Slavicek.
    p. cm. — (Arbitrary borders)
  Audience: Grades 9–12
  Includes bibliographical references and index.
  ISBN 0-7910-8019-6
  1. Great Wall of China (China)—History—Juvenile literature. 2.
China—History—Juvenile literature. I. Title. II. Series.
  DS793.G67S69 2004
  951—dc22
                                        2004010127

Contents

Foreword

Senator **George J. Mitchell**

I spent years working for peace in Northern Ireland and in the Middle East. I also made many visits to the Balkans during the long and violent conflict there.

Each of the three areas is unique; so is each conflict. But there are also some similarities: in each, there are differences over religion, national identity, and territory.

Deep religious differences that lead to murderous hostility are common in human history. Competing aspirations involving national identity are more recent occurrences, but often have been just as deadly.

Territorial disputes—two or more people claiming the same land—are as old as humankind. Almost without exception, such disputes have been a factor in recent conflicts. It is impossible to calculate the extent to which the demand for land—as opposed to religion, national identity, or other factors—figures in the motivation of people caught up in conflict. In my experience it is a substantial factor that has played a role in each of the three conflicts mentioned above.

In Northern Ireland and the Middle East, the location of the border was a major factor in igniting and sustaining the conflict. And it is memorialized in a dramatic and visible way: through the construction of large walls whose purpose is to physically separate the two communities.

In Belfast, the capital and largest city in Northern Ireland, the so-called "Peace Line" cuts through the heart of the city, right across urban streets. Up to thirty feet high in places, topped with barbed wire in others, it is an ugly reminder of the duration and intensity of the conflict.

In the Middle East, as I write these words, the government of Israel has embarked on a huge and controversial effort to construct a security fence roughly along the line that separates Israel from the West Bank.

Having served a tour of duty with the U.S. Army in Berlin, which was once the site of the best known of modern walls, I am skeptical of their long-term value, although they often serve short-term needs. But it cannot be said that such structures represent a new idea. Ancient China built the Great Wall to deter nomadic Mongol tribes from attacking its population.

In much the same way, other early societies established boundaries and fortified them militarily to achieve the goal of self-protection. Borders always have separated people. Indeed, that is their purpose.

This series of books examines the important and timely issue of the significance of arbitrary borders in history. Each volume focuses attention on a territorial division, but the analytical approach is more comprehensive. These studies describe arbitrary borders as places where people interact differently from the way they would if the boundary did not exist. This pattern is especially pronounced where there is no geographic reason for the boundary and no history recognizing its legitimacy. Even though many borders have been defined without legal precision, governments frequently have provided vigorous monitoring and military defense for them.

This series will show how the migration of people and exchange of goods almost always work to undermine the separation that borders seek to maintain. The continuing evolution of a European community provides a contemporary example illustrating this point, most obviously with the adoption of a single currency. Moreover, even former Soviet bloc nations have eliminated barriers to economic and political integration.

Globalization has emerged as one of the most powerful forces in international affairs during the twenty-first century. Not only have markets for the exchange of goods and services become genuinely worldwide, but instant communication and sharing of information have shattered old barriers separating people. Some scholars even argue that globalization has made the entire concept of a territorial nation-state irrelevant. Although the assertion is certainly premature and probably wrong, it highlights the importance of recognizing how borders often have reflected and affirmed the cultural, ethnic, or linguistic perimeters that define a people or a country.

Since the Cold War ended, competition over resources or a variety of interests threaten boundaries more than ever, resulting in contentious interaction, conflict, adaptation, and intermixture. How people define their borders is also a factor in determining how events develop in the surrounding region. This series will provide detailed descriptions of selected arbitrary borders in history with the objective of providing insights on how artificial boundaries separating people will influence international affairs during the next century.

Senator George J. Mitchell
October 2003

Introduction

James I. Matray
California State University, Chico

Throughout history, borders have separated people. Scholars have devoted considerable attention to assessing the significance and impact of territorial boundaries on the course of human history, explaining how they often have been sources of controversy and conflict. In the modern age, the rise of nation-states in Europe created the need for governments to negotiate treaties to confirm boundary lines that periodically changed as a consequence of wars and revolutions. European expansion in the nineteenth century imposed new borders on Africa and Asia. Many native peoples viewed these boundaries as arbitrary and, after independence, continued to contest their legitimacy. At the end of both world wars in the twentieth century, world leaders drew artificial and impermanent lines separating assorted people around the globe. Borders certainly are among the most important factors that have influenced the development of world affairs.

Chelsea House Publishers decided to publish a collection of books looking at arbitrary borders in history in response to the revival of the nuclear crisis in North Korea in October 2002. Recent tensions on the Korean peninsula are a direct consequence of Korea's partition at the 38th parallel at the end of World War II. Other nations in human history have suffered because of similar artificial divisions that have been the result of either international or domestic factors and often a combination of both. In the case of Korea, the United States and the Soviet Union decided in August 1945 to divide the country into two zones of military occupation ostensibly to facilitate the surrender of Japanese forces. However, a political contest was then underway inside Korea to determine the future of the nation after forty years of Japanese colonial rule. The Cold War then created two Koreas with sharply contrasting political, social, and economic systems that symbolized an ideological split among the Korean people. Borders separate people, but rarely prevent their economic, political, social, and cultural interaction. But in Korea, an artificial border has existed since 1945 as a nearly impenetrable barrier precluding meaningful contact between two portions of the same population. Ultimately, two authentic Koreas emerged, exposing how an arbitrary boundary can create circumstances resulting even in the permanent division of a homogeneous people in a historically united land.

Korea's experience in dealing with artificial division may well be unique, but it is not without historical parallels. The first set of books in this series on arbitrary boundaries will provide description and analysis of the division of the Middle East after World War I, the Iron Curtain in Central Europe during the Cold War, the United States-Mexico border, the 17th parallel in Vietnam, and the Mason-Dixon Line. A second set of books will address the Great Wall in China, the Green Line in Israel, and the 38th parallel and demilitarized zone in Korea, and Northern Ireland. Finally, there will be volumes describing how discord over artificial borders in the Louisiana Territory, South Africa, and Czechoslovakia reflected fundamental disputes about sovereignty, religion, and ethnicity. Admittedly, there are many significant differences between these boundaries, but these books will strive to cover as many common themes as possible. In so doing, each will help readers conceptualize how complex factors such as colonialism, culture, and economics determine the nature of contact between people along these borders. Although globalization has emerged as a powerful force working against the creation and maintenance of lines separating people, boundaries likely will endure as factors having a persistent influence on world events. This series of books will provide insights about the impact of arbitrary borders on human history and how such borders continue to shape the modern world.

James I. Matray
Chico, California
April 2004

1

China's Legendary Northern Wall

Legend has it that China's most famous landmark owes its existence to a dream. According to Chinese folklore, one night more than 2,000 years ago, Qin Shi Huang Di, the first ruler of the newly unified Chinese Empire, dreamt that he journeyed to the moon on an enchanted carpet. From the emperor's vantage point high above the Earth, his huge new realm appeared vulnerable. Towering mountain ranges guarded the kingdom's western frontier, the broad Yangzi River cut off any potential invaders from the south, and the Yellow Sea shielded the east. Only China's long border with the arid steppes (grasslands) and deserts of Inner Asia—and the fierce tribal horsemen who inhabited them—looked alarmingly exposed. No geographical barrier, Qin Shi Huang Di noted anxiously, defined China's northern frontier. To the empire's north, nature had neglected to provide any great bodies of water or lofty mountain ranges to safeguard his fledgling domain.

The very next morning the emperor summoned his most trusted general and commanded him to create an artificial separation between Inner Asia's steppes and China's fertile farm fields where a natural one had never existed. Thus was born the Great Wall of China: the biggest defensive project in the history of humankind. Meandering for some 2,000 miles along the wide transition zone of infertile land between the Chinese Empire's well-watered valleys and plains and Inner Asia's parched expanses, the Great Wall would form an arbitrary line of earth and stone between a country that was "cultivated, in the double sense of agriculture and civilization" and what Qin Shi Huang Di considered as the menacing wastelands of the north.[1]

The story of Qin Shi Huang Di's dream is just one of many legends that have evolved about the Great Wall since construction began on the mammoth barrier some 22 centuries ago. Perhaps the best known of these legends is that the Great Wall is the only manmade structure visible from the moon. Even though astronauts have been saying for years that all that can be made out is the turquoise of the Earth's oceans, the gold of its vast deserts, and here and there, a green patch of vegetation, this

The Great Wall of China, parts of which are more than 2,000 years old, is a structure with many branches and sections. Depending on what is considered part of the Wall, the length is given as from 2,000 to 4,000 miles long. This photograph shows a portion of the wall in Beijing, China.

claim has been repeated in countless books and articles on the wall right up to the present day. Another long-standing myth about the Great Wall, as historian Arthur Waldron has noted, is that the wall marked a single, unchanging northern boundary line for imperial China throughout the empire's more than 2,000-year existence (221 B.C.–A.D. 1912). In truth, the Great Wall is not a single, unified structure but rather a conglomeration of ramparts and towers that were repeatedly repositioned by a succession of rulers, each of whom had his own conception of just how far the empire's political control should reach beyond the Chinese heartland. For example, the dynamic "Martial Emperor" Wu Di (141–87 B.C.) extended the wall for hundreds of miles to the west of Qin Shi Huang Di's original ramparts, reflecting his expansionist ambitions in Central Asia. Many of Wu Di's successors held a much narrower vision of where their domains should end, however. Thus the emperors of the Ming ruling family (1368–1644), the wall's last builders, positioned large segments of their Great Wall significantly to the east and south of earlier border fortifications. In sharp contrast to the defensiveness and closure that characterized Ming policy toward the steppe, under China's final dynasty, the Manchu Qing (1644–1912), the empire's frontiers stretched deep into the arid plains of Inner Asia. The Great Wall completely lost its purpose, both as a military defense line and as a national boundary.

Controversy as well as myth surrounds the Great Wall. Historians have long disagreed regarding the actual effectiveness of China's famed monument as a defense line. Many consider the huge fortifications as a colossal waste of money and manpower. They point out that in spite of the Great Wall, the Chinese Empire suffered numerous invasions from the north, including two—by the Mongols in the thirteenth century and the Manchu in the seventeenth century—that resulted in the entire country falling under foreign rule for lengthy periods. The Great Wall, they argue, proved no more effective in protecting the Chinese from their northern enemies than the heavily fortified Maginot Line, built by the French on their border with Germany after World War I, proved in shielding the Republic from Hitler's armies during World War II. Other scholars, however, counter that during those times when it was adequately manned and maintained by China's imperial government, the wall served well against the sudden attacks of Inner Asia's lightning-fast, mounted warriors. If the wall had never been erected, they assert, the empire would have suffered continual incursions from the warlike tribes to its north rather than only a few major invasions over the course of two millennia.

The exact size and route of China's great northern defense line has also been much debated among scholars. Although the wall's length is often given as about 2,000 miles, some scholars believe that the structure is closer to 4,000 miles long if all its various branches and secondary sections, many of which have yet to be surveyed, are included. Experts disagree as well regarding the precise course followed by the Great Wall before China's final bout of wall building during the Ming dynasty. Centuries of wind, rain, snow, and desert sandstorms have obliterated the majority of the mostly earthen wall sections constructed by dynasties before the Ming, and much archaeological work remains to be done on those crumbling portions that have managed to survive Mother Nature's onslaughts.

Until recently, China's communist regime, in power since 1949, had neither the funds nor the inclination to support extensive archaeological research in the nation. Today, there is probably no other place on earth where major archaeological findings are emerging as rapidly as in the People's Republic of China. The Great Wall, China's chief tourist attraction and its unofficial national symbol since the early twentieth century, has been the focus of much of this remarkable archaeological activity. As new discoveries regarding the Great Wall are revealed, our understanding of the massive structure and its origins, functions, and significance—both as a political border and a military defense line—continues to grow. Consequently, the story of the arbitrary line of stone and earth first drawn by Qin Shi Huang Di more than 2,000 years ago to separate China's rich farmlands from the arid steppes of Inner Asia is still very much in the process of unfolding.

2

Before the
Great Wall

W alls have been a part of the Chinese landscape for a very long time. Archeological evidence indicates that the Chinese began erecting thick earthen walls around their settlements well over 3,000 years ago.

A ZEAL FOR WALLS

By the beginning of the first millennium B.C., walls had become an essential feature of virtually every Chinese town and village. Indeed, in the Chinese language, "the same word [cheng] means either a city or a city wall; you cannot have one without the other," observes one scholar of ancient China.[2]

In building walls around their communities, the ancient Chinese were by no means unique. Prehistoric civilizations all over the world enclosed their settlements with ramparts of earth or stone as a defense against wild animals and looters. "Yet," as historian Jonathan Fryer has noted, "no other civilization seems to have adopted walls as enthusiastically as the Chinese."[3] The people of ancient China displayed a genuine passion for wall building, walling off not just their towns but also their palaces, houses, farm fields, and temples. According to Fryer:

> They even projected their wall-consciousness beyond the realm of the mortal world into the kingdom of the gods, whose cities and palaces were also surrounded by walls. The God of Walls and Moats is himself an important figure in the divine hierarchy whose territory is not only the dividing line between the secure inside and the dark world outside but also that between Life and Death.[4]

It was the God of Walls and Moats who informed a dying person that his time had finally come, the Chinese believed. His two half-human, half-beast assistants guided the departing soul to the great hall on the frontiers of the underworld that separated the earthly from the spiritual realm.

The inclination of the ancient Chinese to wall off just about everything seems all the more remarkable in light of the arduous process they used to construct their walls. Most of the early

Chinese walls were built using the exhausting and time-consuming *hang-tu* or pounded earth method. Laborers started by fashioning the form or mold for the new wall: a large wooden or bamboo frame whose sides were set as far apart as the preferred width of the wall. Next they dug up great quantities of earth and hauled it to the frame. After dumping the dirt into the form, the workers stamped on the earth with their feet or used wooden tools to ram it into a dense layer no more than half a foot thick. This backbreaking procedure was repeated layer upon layer as the structure slowly rose, a mere four to six inches at a time. When the hang-tu wall had finally attained a certain desired height, the workers removed the wooden form and lugged it to the next segment of the structure where they started the tiring process of dumping and pounding the loose earth all over again.

A NEW KIND OF WALL: THE INTER-KINGDOM RAMPARTS

Wall building in China entered a new era around the middle of the first millennium B.C. Previously, walls had been constructed to safeguard a particular town, household, religious shrine, or agricultural field. Now the Chinese began raising walls to safeguard entire kingdoms.

During the early first millennium B.C., dozens of small principalities arose within the Chinese heartland—roughly the same area that makes up the eastern and central portions of the modern People's Republic of China (PRC). Over time, the noble rulers of the various Chinese states became increasingly militaristic, devoting ever more of their resources to raising and outfitting big private armies. By the 700s B.C., the boldest and most ambitious of the local leaders were using their large new armies to bolster their political and economic power by wresting territory from bordering kingdoms.

Desperate to protect their domains against predatory neighbors, many regional rulers turned to the same defensive strategy on which they had long relied to protect their cities and palaces: wall building. According to some ancient Chinese sources, the kingdom of Chu was the first Chinese state to attempt to protect

In the first millennium B.C., mounted nomads roamed Inner Asia, relying on their flocks for almost all of their basic needs. The nomads sometimes used violent means to acquire any other goods they needed, and many historians believe this prompted the construction of the border fortifications that preceded the Great Wall.

its territory by walling off aggressive neighbors. Chu's rulers began constructing what the ancient chroniclers referred to as chang cheng ("long walls") along its boundaries sometime around the mid-seventh century B.C. These long walls were to serve as protection against two formidable rivals: the kingdom of Qin to the north and west and the kingdom of Qi to the northeast. Over the course of the next 200 years, a host of other states, including Chu's powerful neighbors Qin and Qi, would follow Chu's lead and raise inter-kingdom fortifications where no natural barriers such as mountains or rivers existed. Even the tiny kingdom of Zhongshan in north central China managed to erect its own chang cheng.

The inter-kingdom walls were of varying lengths with the

longest stretching across the open countryside for more than 2,000 li. (The "li" is an ancient Chinese unit of measure equal to approximately one-third of a mile; hence, 2,000 li equals approximately 670 miles.) When available, stone was used to construct the ramparts. Most often, the laborers used the slow and arduous hang-tu method to fashion their states' new artificial barriers from earth, the one building material that was always at hand.

Whereas soldiers carried out most of the work on the inter-kingdom defense lines, rulers also drafted thousands of civilians to toil on the walls. A ballad dating from the 600s and recorded in the ancient Chinese classic, the Book of Odes, reflects the mood of the hapless peasants forced to abandon their families and farms for months at a time to slave on their kingdoms' far-flung border fortifications:

> Long ago when we started,
> The wine-millet and cooking-millet
> were in flower.
> Now that we are on the march again
> Snow falls upon the mire.
> The King's service brings many hardships.
> We have no time to rest or bide.
> We do indeed long to return . . .[5]

Despite the considerable hardships that the Chinese people endured in raising the border ramparts, the new defense systems failed to bring peace to their violence-ridden homeland. The manmade barriers crisscrossing China's heartland "were only of minimal defensive effectiveness," explained Fryer, "as the enemy found it relatively easy to outflank them."[6] Indeed, from the fifth century to the late third century B.C., the so-called Warring States period in Chinese history, the internal strife that had plagued China since the 700s B.C. intensified as a half dozen of the largest kingdoms invaded and absorbed their weaker rivals. The incessant fighting took a terrible toll on the Chinese. Tens of thousands were slaughtered; in some areas, entire villages were wiped out. It was becoming increasingly evident that the bloodshed would stop only when one kingdom proved able to vanquish all its competitors, abolish the arbitrary borders that divided one Chinese state from another, and unite the war-weary Chinese people under a single rule.

THE NORTHERN BORDER RAMPARTS: WALLING OFF THE INNER ASIANS

During the tumultuous Warring States period in Chinese history, three kingdoms—Qin in the northwest, Zhao in the north, and Yan in the northeast—did not merely erect chang cheng to protect their territories from other Chinese states. These three powerful states also sought to wall off their non-Chinese neighbors to the north, a nomadic people whose culture and economic practices were very different from their own. The frontier fortifications erected by Yan, Qin, and Zhao to seal off their northern frontiers from the nomads were destined to play a critical role in Chinese history. In time, this complex of walls and other defensive structures would be linked together to form large portions of China's first "great" wall, the Great Wall of the first emperor of a united China, Qin Shi Huang Di.

Yan, Zhao, and Qin's northern neighbors lived in the southernmost reaches of the geographical region known as Inner Asia. Although it also contains forests, mountain ranges, and deserts, Inner Asia is largely composed of grassy, semi-arid steppes or plains. The core of Inner Asia consists of three regions. Eastern Inner Asia encompasses Manchuria, today the far northeastern portion of the People's Republic of China, including Heilongjiang, Jilin, and Liaoning provinces. Central Inner Asia comprises the modern Autonomous Regions of Inner Mongolia and Ningxia, which, like Manchuria, were once independent of China and today are part of the PRC, and the Mongolian Republic, an independent nation bordered to the south and west by the PRC and to the north by the Russian Federation. Western Inner Asia, the last of three regions, is composed of the huge modern-day

Xinjiang Uighur Autonomous Region in the north and Tibet in the south. Like the Ningxia and Inner Mongolia Autonomous Regions, Xinjiang is firmly controlled by the PRC even though the term "autonomous" suggests a large degree of self-rule.

Although only traces of the northern walls have survived into the modern era, the available archeological evidence suggests that the governments of Zhao, Qin, and Yan went to an enormous amount of trouble and expense to construct barriers between themselves and the Inner Asians. In addition to their chang cheng, the new northern defenses featured garrisons, watchtowers, lookout platforms, and other structures. Another common feature of Qin, Zhao, and Yan's carefully engineered frontier defenses, as historian Nicola Di Cosmo has noted, "was that they constituted an integrated system of fortifications that included not only manufactured structures but also natural barriers. These lines of fortifications made extensive use of the natural features of the surrounding topography."[7] Accordingly, in mountainous areas where natural obstacles such as ravines, precipices, or narrow gullies could be counted on to repel invading armies, manmade structures "may have been limited to a few lookout posts."[8] Where such geographical barriers did not exist, however, the three states created their own artificial partitions—arbitrary and heavily fortified borderlines of stone and pounded earth.

SETTING THE STAGE FOR THE NORTHERN WALLS: THE RISE OF TRUE NOMADISM IN INNER ASIA

The traditional explanation for the origin of Qin, Zhao, and Yan's elaborate northern defense lines centers on nomadic raids on Chinese villages. According to this long-accepted version of the walls' roots, the rulers of the three northern kingdoms erected their frontier ramparts for purely defensive reasons. They wanted to safeguard their states' northernmost farming settlements in the wake of a rash of hit-and-run attacks by marauding bands of nomads from the Inner Asian steppe.

Most scholars agree that "true" or full-fledged nomads were

scarce in the vast grasslands of Inner Asia until approximately the middle of the first millennium B.C.—around the same time that Qin, Zhao, and Yan began constructing their northern fortifications.[9] True nomads are people who have no fixed home. Instead, they wander from one place to another, according to the food supply. Before the fifth or sixth century B.C., most of the various non-Chinese groups who populated Inner Asia were seminomadic. Typically, these early inhabitants of the steppe were part-time farmers who tended their fields and resided in settled communities for many months at a stretch.

Because eking a living out of the dry soil of the steppe was a constant struggle, the residents of ancient Inner Asia supplemented their agricultural activities with livestock herding. To keep their flocks of sheep, cattle, goats, and horses well fed and healthy, they spent part of every year on the move, rotating among several different pasture grounds as rainfall and climate dictated, a practice referred to as pastoral nomadism. The herdsmen and their families traveled in units called bands or clans organized around kinship and marital ties. To avoid overgrazing a particular area, these herding units were compact—the average nomadic band consisted of fewer than 10 families. The little groups of wanderers lived simply, sleeping in tents fashioned from animal skins or felt and carrying few possessions with them.

For many centuries, Inner Asians relied successfully on a mixed economy, practicing both agriculture and pastoral nomadism. By the time of the Warring States period when the first northern ramparts were being raised by the kingdoms of Qin, Yan, and Zhao, however, an important shift had taken place in the grassy plains to the north of China. More and more of the steppe inhabitants were abandoning farming and a settled existence altogether for a completely mobile way of life.

Historians and anthropologists can only guess at the reasons for this change from semi-nomadism to true nomadism. Some scholars have linked the shift to a fully nomadic economy and society in Inner Asia to increased contacts between the region's residents and nomadic groups who lived to their north and west in the steppes of Eurasia. Others have emphasized climatic changes in trying to explain the rise of full-fledged nomadism in the Inner Asian steppe during the mid-first millennium B.C., theorizing that the region became significantly more arid around that time—a phenomenon known as aridization. Without adequate rainfall for growing the millet (a type of grain) and other agricultural crops that had once formed a vital part of their diet, the people of the steppe had little choice but to become full-time herdsmen. To ensure a steady supply of fodder for the flocks on which they now relied entirely for their sustenance, the Inner Asians reconciled themselves to a wholly nomadic existence, wandering continually from one pastureland to another according to the changing seasons and the availability of fresh grass and water.

Whether the economic and social transformation that occurred in the vast prairies bordering northern China around the mid-first millennium B.C. resulted from cultural interactions with other nomadic peoples, aridization of the climate, or a combination of both factors remains a matter of debate among scholars. There is, however, one point on which most scholars can agree: the Inner Asians' ability to adopt a full-fledged nomadic lifestyle was closely linked to their developing skills as horsemen.

Wild horses are exceptionally difficult to tame and many anthropologists believe it was not until about the fifth or sixth century B.C. that Inner Asians were able to develop the techniques required to control these high-spirited animals. Once they had finally mastered the art of horseback riding, the herdsmen of the steppe could cover far greater distances than ever before in the ongoing quest for fresh grass and water for their flocks. Moreover, fewer herdsmen could now manage significantly larger numbers of animals. With the rise of horsemanship in Inner Asia, an economy based totally on herding as opposed to a mixed economy marked by both farming and herding had become a genuine option for the region's inhabitants.

STEPPE NOMADS VERSUS CHINESE FARMERS AND THE ORIGINS OF THE NORTHERN WALLS

Inner Asia's "true" or full-fledged mounted nomads relied on their flocks for more than just meat, dairy products, and transportation. They also fashioned their clothing and tents from the hides, wool, and fur of the beasts that they herded and hunted in the steppe. A remarkably resourceful people, the nomads used the native animals of the steppe to fulfill most of their basic needs for food, warmth, and shelter.

In spite of their resourcefulness, the inhabitants of the Inner Asian steppe were not entirely self-sufficient. Abandoning farming and a settled life for a completely mobile existence meant that they now found it difficult—if not impossible—to produce essential agricultural and manufactured goods such as grain and metal. Many scholars have argued that these economic shortfalls faced by the full-fledged nomads of the steppe from about the mid-first millennium B.C. onward were of utmost importance to the evolution of the Great Wall. These historians contend that it was the violent tactics the nomads sometimes used to acquire the goods they needed that provided the catalyst for the construction of the Great Wall's forerunners, the northern border fortifications of Yan, Zhao, and Qin.

In attempting to make up for their economic deficiencies, it was perhaps inevitable that the nomads should turn their gaze southward toward the Chinese heartland. Just to the south of the steppe in northern China, where the soil was richer and the climate significantly wetter than in Inner Asia, farming and the sedentary lifestyle that inevitably goes along with an agricultural economy flourished. Consequently, the goods that the steppe peoples most desired but could not produce for themselves because of their nomadic lifestyle—manufactured items such as cloth, metal, and ceramic utensils and agricultural items such as millet and other grains—were readily available in the workshops and farm fields that dotted the northern Chinese states of Qin, Zhao, and Yan.

Both ancient written sources and recent archaeological findings indicate that the nomads of the steppe were generally able to obtain the products they sought from the settled farmers and artisans of northern China through trade. In exchange for Chinese grains, cloth, and handicrafts, the herders of the Inner Asian grasslands offered animal products such as wool, fur, and livestock, including sheep, cattle, and horses.

As a rule, the nomads traded peacefully with their sedentary neighbors, but when the Chinese rebuffed their offers to barter or when their herds had been reduced by illness or drought, the Inner Asians were ready and willing to use force to get what they wanted. Highly skilled at archery as well as horsemanship, they had both the military expertise and the mobility needed to be successful raiders. Indeed, the Chinese farmers could do little to protect themselves from the small bands of armed steppe nomads who swept down without warning on their communities. After raiding the villagers' grain supplies and carrying off whatever else happened to catch their fancy, the fast-riding horsemen would scatter and melt into the vast grasslands before local authorities even had a chance to muster their defense forces. Needless to say, the nomads' hit-and-run attacks "hardly promoted friendly relations or sympathy" between the Inner Asian and Chinese peoples. "Agriculturists saw nomads as bullies who preferred taking from others to working for their living," whereas the nomads "looked on Chinese farmers as weaklings."[10]

A NOVEL THEORY FOR THE NORTHERN WALLS' ORIGIN: AN OFFENSIVE STRATEGY

Without doubt, nomadic raiding caused a great deal of suffering among the residents of China's northernmost farming communities. Whether the governments of Yan, Qin, and Zhao were sufficiently troubled by the nomads' sporadic hit-and-run attacks to erect elaborate and costly fortifications along their northern frontiers with the steppe is another question altogether. Is it reasonable to believe, as scholars have traditionally argued, that these three kingdoms would have invested the time and labor of thousands of soldiers and civilians to construct walls whose sole purpose was to stop small bands of horsemen from looting their border villages now and then? The day would come when many of the steppe's scattered tribes would unite into vast military confederations capable of posing a grave threat indeed to the Chinese people and their government. In the mid-first millennium B.C. when the northern border fortifications were being erected, however, that day was still many years in the future. Not until after the end of the Warring States period around 200 B.C. would the steppe nomads systematically begin to organize themselves into groups larger than the small, loosely linked units that they traditionally used for herding and hunting (and occasionally for raiding).

One scholar who does not accept the conventional view that China's earliest northern fortification lines were the product of tensions between Chinese farmers and marauding nomadic horsemen is Nicola Di Cosmo. In his recent study of early Chinese-nomadic relations, *Ancient China and its Enemies: The Rise of Nomadic Power in East Asian History*, Di Cosmo looked at the forerunners of the first Great Wall from a fresh perspective. He argued that the northern barricades created by the governments of Yan, Qin, and Zhao must be understood within the political and military context of the turbulent period in Chinese history when they were built. According to Di Cosmo, only by viewing these elaborate artificial barriers in relation to the bitter inter-kingdom power struggles of the Warring States era when their construction was being planned and carried out can we hope to identify the walls' true roots and purposes.

Throughout the two centuries of the Warring States period, China's various states were locked in a vicious, no-holds-barred contest for supremacy and survival. In hopes of boosting their states' military, political, and economic resources and influence, many of the rival Chinese governments sought to expand their rule into neighboring territories. As the extensive inter-kingdom walls of the Warring States era demonstrate, the territories that these ambitious rulers coveted typically belonged to other

Chinese states. As part of their relentless campaign to increase their own states' resources and power, however, some of the kingdoms on the periphery of the Chinese heartland also sought to expand beyond China's traditional borders into lands inhabited by non-Chinese peoples. Di Cosmo maintained that it was this obsession of the warring kingdoms with "state aggrandizement," whether at the expense of Chinese or non-Chinese neighbors, rather than nomadic raiding, that actually spurred the construction of the northern ramparts of Qin, Yan, and Zhao.[11]

Shortly before Qin, Yan, and Zhao erected their fortifications, the three kingdoms' armies had made forays into the grassy plains to the north of the Chinese heartland. The chief motivation of the states' rulers for sending troops into these alien areas was not to punish nomadic raiders but rather to acquire new territories, territories they hoped would give their kingdom an edge over competitors in the ongoing struggle for control of China. Once they had subjugated or driven away the northern territories' long-time nomadic inhabitants, Di Cosmo has speculated, the three kingdoms set about creating heavily fortified new boundaries to protect the conquered lands from horsemen intent on reclaiming what they considered as their own.

> In other words, Qin, Yan, and Zhao needed to protect themselves from the nomads only after they had taken large portions of territory from [them] and had chased the nomads away from their homelands. Surely at some point the fortifications did acquire a "defensive" function, but the context suggests strongly that this defensive role was subordinated to a grander strategy, one that was militarily offensive and territorially expansive, pursued by all three Chinese states.[12]

A HIGHLY ARBITRARY BORDER

In developing his theory that ruthless Chinese expansionism—rather than nomadic attacks on innocent Chinese farmers—spurred the building of the northern ramparts, Di Cosmo drew on the most up-to-date archaeological findings. For years following the establishment of the People's Republic of China in 1949, the nation's communist leadership took only a limited interest in promoting archaeological and historical research in their country. During the last two decades of the twentieth century, however, the PRC's leaders began to place new emphasis on China's rich cultural heritage as a means of bolstering national pride and unity. One consequence of the communist regime's belated appreciation for China's past has been greater governmental support for archaeological fieldwork at sites across the nation. For the first time, Chinese scientists have been able to carry out extensive excavations near the largely eroded northern walls of the ancient states of Qin, Zhao, and Yan.

These recent excavations of the ruined Warring States fortifications and of the countryside surrounding them suggest that the northern boundaries established by Qin, Zhao, and Yan were highly arbitrary. The walls "did not mark an ecological boundary," Di Cosmo has noted, "that is, the walls were not built to separate steppe and sown, nomad and farmer."[13] Indeed, researchers have determined that large sections of the ramparts were located in the middle of semi-arid grasslands, miles from the well-watered agricultural fields of Qin, Zhao, and Yan that the walls were supposed to be protecting. Moreover, with the exception of a few items that obviously belonged to the Chinese occupying armies assigned to patrol the fortifications, all the cultural artifacts that have thus far been recovered near the walls are of Inner Asian origin. In light of these archaeological discoveries, it would be hard to escape the conclusion that the northern bulwarks of Qin, Zhao, and Yan formed very arbitrary borders indeed since substantial segments of the barriers appear to have been erected well within traditional nomadic territory. "Certainly," according to Di Cosmo has written, the walls had not been built 'in between' Chinese and nomads, "but instead ran through an alien land inhabited by alien groups.[14]

BORROWING FROM THE STEPPE NOMADS:
THE RISE OF THE CHINESE CAVALRY

In attempting to explain why the three northern Chinese states sought to expand their boundaries into the "alien land" of the steppe in the first place and were then willing to go through the considerable effort of heavily fortifying their new arbitrary borders with the nomads, Di Cosmo has pointed to an important shift in Chinese military strategy during the Warring States period. Although the grasslands enclosed by the new fortifications would have made poor farm fields, they were ideally suited for another purpose—the breeding and pasturing of warhorses. It was precisely at this juncture in their ongoing contest for control of the Chinese heartland that the feuding "Chinese states began to pay attention to cavalry and to the use of mounted warfare." [15]

Interestingly, the Chinese got the idea for mounted warfare from their nomadic enemies in the north. Chinese armies had long used horse-drawn chariots in battle, but it was not until the Warring States period that they began putting their soldiers on horseback. The first warring state to use mounted troops was the northern state of Zhao, which encompassed much of the present-day Chinese province of Shanxi. Zhao's ruler, King Wuling (325–299 B.C.), deeply admired the military skills and riding expertise of the nomadic horsemen who resided on the outskirts of his domain. Persuaded that the nomads' ability to move swiftly from place to place and shoot with bows from horseback made them exceptional fighters, Wuling vowed to add cavalry units to his own army. According to an ancient Chinese chronicle, Wuling, in 307 B.C., informed his surprised advisors that he intended to copy not just the fighting tactics of the steppe horsemen but also their costumes of trousers and short tunics—more practical riding apparel than the flowing robes traditionally worn by all Chinese who did not labor in the fields. "I propose to adopt the horseman's clothing of the non-Chinese nomads and will teach my people their mounted archery—and how the world will talk!" he reputedly declared.[16]

THE END OF THE WARRING STATES PERIOD

The turbulent Warring States period finally ended in 221 B.C. when the kingdom of Qin managed to overcome Zhao, Yan, and all the rest of its competitor states and unite China into a single empire. Qin's rise had begun with a succession of conquests of bordering states in the late fourth century that picked up momentum under the command of the youthful and ambitious King Zheng, nicknamed the "Tiger of Qin."

After annexing Qin's last remaining rival, the kingdom of Qi, in 221 B.C., Zheng boldly crowned himself Qin Shi Huang Di, the First Sovereign Emperor of the Chinese Empire and the founder of the Qin dynasty. That accomplished, Qin Shi Huang Di devoted himself to consolidating his control over his vast new realm, which he and his millions of new subjects knew not as China but as Zhongguo—the Middle Kingdom. (The early Chinese may have adopted this name for their homeland because they thought it was located at the earth's geographical center. Our name for China is actually derived from the name "Qin," which is pronounced "chin" in English). In the process of cementing his authority over his far-flung domain, the First Sovereign Emperor would radically transform the world of ancient China, initiating a host of sweeping political, social, and economic reforms as well as a remarkable array of ambitious construction schemes. The most enduring—and controversial—of Qin Shi Huang Di's massive building projects proved to be the formidable defense line that he erected along his new empire's northern frontier, an arbitrary border of stone and earth that future generations would dub the Great Wall of China.

3

China's First Great Wall: The Wall of Qin Shi Huang Di

On assuming his exalted new title of First Sovereign Emperor of the Chinese Empire in 221 B.C., Qin Shi Huang Di immediately proclaimed a series of far-reaching political, economic, and social reforms. These measures were designed both to enhance Qin Shi Huang Di's own power and to strengthen and knit together his sprawling new domain.

THE EMPEROR CONSOLIDATES HIS POWER:
MELTING WEAPONS AND BURNING BOOKS

In cementing his control over the newly unified Middle Kingdom, Qin Shi Huang Di's first objective was to break the power of the aristocrats who had ruled the various Chinese states. With that goal in mind, the emperor promptly dissolved all of the conquered states and created his own arbitrary internal borders for China, dividing the heartland into 36 provinces directed by officials who served strictly at his bidding. To prevent the deposed rulers of the former states or their supporters from organizing rebellions, the emperor forbade the private ownership of arms. Imperial authorities confiscated thousands of bronze swords, spears, and other weapons, melting them down to make a dozen giant statues to adorn the courtyard of Qin Shi Huang Di's magnificent palace at his capital, Xianyang (near the modern city of Xi'an in Shanxi province). Grimly determined to stave off all potential threats to his rule from within China, the First Sovereign Emperor also forced 120,000 of the defeated kingdoms' richest and most powerful families to move to Xianyang where he could keep a watchful eye on their every move.

Qin Shi Huang Di further sought to tighten his control over his subjects by stringently monitoring their access to books and knowledge. In 213 B.C., he decreed that all writings in the empire be confiscated and burned with the exception of manuals on "useful" topics such as farming, medicine, law, and divination (foretelling the future by supernatural means).[17] He was particularly concerned with destroying all works that praised the moral values or political systems of the past, such as the writings

The first emperor of China, Qin Shi Huang Di, seen here, came to power in 221 B.C. He enacted many reforms to strengthen his empire and increase his power and created the earliest version of what would become the Great Wall.

of the fifth century B.C. philosopher Confucius and his disciples. Any person who dared to defy the emperor's tyrannical new policy faced exile or worse. According to some ancient Chinese chronicles, Qin Shi Huang Di went so far as to have 460 Confucian scholars buried alive for refusing to hand over their books to government authorities.

Not content to impose intellectual uniformity on the Chinese people, Qin Shi Huang Di resolved to impose economic uniformity on his subjects as well. He standardized all weights and measures throughout the empire and replaced the many different kinds of money used by the Warring States kingdoms with a single currency. In hopes of improving communication among the Middle Kingdom's 36 far-flung provinces, the emperor also standardized and simplified the characters used in Chinese writing. Although a multitude of different dialects continued to be spoken in the various parts of the empire, by enforcing a single standardized script Qin Shi Huang Di was at least able to ensure a written foundation for understanding among the Chinese people. To make sure that his new policies were followed, Qin Shi Huang Di decreed that any person caught using local forms of script, weights, or money would be charged with treason against the Chinese Empire.

KNITTING THE EMPIRE TOGETHER: BUILDING ROADS AND TEARING DOWN WALLS

Qin Shi Huang Di's determination to weld the former warring states together was further reflected in the ambitious public works projects he initiated. Hundreds of thousands of Chinese were conscripted to excavate canals and build more than 4,700 miles of roads. Fanning out in all directions from his capital at Xianyang, Qin Shi Huang Di's vast new highway system rivaled that of the ancient Roman Empire. Painstakingly laid out in straight lines of a uniform width, the new thoroughfares were intended not only to encourage communication among the different parts of the Middle Kingdom but also to facilitate the movements of the huge imperial army.

The First Sovereign Emperor set his subjects to work knocking down the old as well as building the new as part of his ongoing crusade to bring China together. Convinced that the ramparts were impediments to communication and effective administration within the empire, he drafted peasants from all over his realm to demolish city walls and large sections of the inter-kingdom fortifications erected by the rival governments of the Warring States era. "The sovereign emperor has extended his rule," observed one Chinese chronicler. "He has thrown down and destroyed the inner and other walls.... He has leveled all obstacles and removed all difficulties."[18] Aside from promoting the centralization of the Chinese Empire by leveling "all obstacles," the emperor probably had another motive for destroying the old inter-kingdom defensive systems. Ever anxious to safeguard his own power, Qin Shi Huang Di may have sought to ensure that these imposing complexes of walls, watchtowers, and forts would never fall into the hands of his opponents.

QIN SHI HUANG DI AND THE NORTHERN FRONTIER WALLS

Qin Shi Huang Di was eager to tear down most of the defensive walls erected by the various kingdoms of the pre-imperial era, but he did not want to eliminate all of them. The northern frontier ramparts built by Zhao, Yan, and his home state of Qin during the Warring States period still served an important purpose, Qin Shi Huang Di believed, and should be spared. Indeed, the emperor was prepared to do much more than just preserve these northern fortifications. He wanted to significantly strengthen the aging defense systems by repairing their walls and towers and linking them with many miles of new construction into one continuous structure. In the process of restoring and consolidating the ramparts of the three northern "warring states," Qin Shi Huang Di would create the earliest incarnation of what eventually came to be known as the Great Wall of China.

Since only scattered remnants of the original construction have survived into modern times, the precise length of Qin Shi Huang Di's northern defense line is unknown. Most modern scholars, however, believe that the Middle Kingdom's first Great Wall was at least 1,500 miles in length, stretching from Liaodong near the Yellow Sea all the way west to the modern Chinese province of Gansu. If the one ancient Chinese chronicle that discusses the structure in any detail—Shiji or Records of the Grand Historian by the first-century B.C. scholar Sima Qian—is to be believed, the Great Wall of Qin Shi Huang Di was even longer. According to Sima Qian, the complex of walls, signal towers, and forts that composed the First Sovereign Emperor's great barricade extended for "more than 10,000 li" (over 3,300 miles).[19]

Like the earlier walls of Qin, Yan, and Zhao that it incorporated, the first Great Wall formed an arbitrary boundary between the realm of the Inner Asian tribes and that of the Chinese. In some places it stayed well within the wide transition zone of infertile land between the arid northern steppes and the fertile farmlands of China's heartland; in other areas it veered into grasslands traditionally inhabited by nomads. The arbitrary nature of Qin Shi Huang Di's new and improved border with China's northern neighbors is particularly evident in a region generally known as the Ordos.

QIN SHI HUANG DI AND THE ORDOS

According to the Records of the Grand Historian, directly before ordering the creation of what later generations of Chinese would dub his Wan Li Chang Cheng ("The Long Wall of 10,000 Li"), Qin Shi Huang Di launched a major military campaign into nomad-held territories to the north of the Chinese heartland. Somewhere between about 220 and 215 B.C.—historians differ regarding the exact year—the First Sovereign Emperor commanded General Meng Tian to assemble an army of 300,000 to attack the nomadic tribes of the Ordos—the lands within the Yellow River's great northwestern bend. Qin Shi Huang Di's objective in this campaign, Sima Qian wrote, was to "drive out" the nomads and "take over the territory to the south of the Yellow River" and inside the river's wide loop.[20]

Northern China's major river, the Yellow River or Huang He, originates in the modern-day Chinese province of Qinghai. From Qinghai, it meanders northeastward through Gansu province and the Ningxia Autonomous Region. Leaving Ningxia, the river flows northward into the Inner Mongolia Autonomous Region. On reaching central Inner Mongolia, the Huang He changes direction twice, first flowing sharply eastward, then dropping southward toward present-day Shanxi province. In the process, it forms a big upside-down "∩"—the Yellow River loop. Today, the Ordos—as the territory enclosed within the arch is generally called—is divided between the Inner Mongolia and Ningxia Autonomous Regions.

Ecologically, the region within the bend of the Yellow River "is mixed." [21] In the loop's northernmost section, the Huang He flows through a fertile plain well suited to farming. Directly below and completely bounded by the arch of the Yellow River lies the vast Ordos Desert for which the region is named. Although considered as the southernmost fringe of the vast Gobi Desert, the Ordos is not what most people would think of on hearing the word "desert." Parts of the Ordos are extremely arid and barren, yet the region also contains large grass-covered plains that receive enough rainfall to make fine pasturage. Clearly, the Ordos had potential value for the Chinese Empire as farming and grazing land. Probably even more important to the emperor, the territory enclosed within the Yellow River loop possessed significant strategic value because its southernmost portions lay uncomfortably close to the political heart of his empire—the capital city of Xianyang.

Nearly a century before Qin Shi Huang Di ordered Meng Tian to conquer the territory within the Yellow River arch for the new Chinese Empire, another Chinese ruler had also coveted the Ordos. He was King Wuling of the northwestern kingdom of Zhao—the same monarch who had borrowed the idea for mounted warfare from his nomadic neighbors in the steppe. With the assistance of his new cavalry units, Wuling pushed into the territory enclosed by the Yellow River bend and chased out its long-time nomadic inhabitants. That accomplished, he promptly ordered the construction of earthen chang cheng and other fortifications just to the north of the Yellow River's great arch to safeguard his new territorial conquests. As the inter-state strife of the Warring States period intensified over the course of the third century B.C., however, Wuling's successors were apparently too preoccupied with their powerful Chinese rivals to pay much heed to their kingdom's northern territories. Consequently, by the time that Qin Shi Huang Di had defeated Zhao and the rest of his Chinese rivals to create the first unified Chinese state, most of the Ordos had been reclaimed by nomadic herdsmen.

Even though by rights the grassy plains of the Ordos "should have belonged to the steppe," notes one historian, concerned as always with augmenting his own power and that of his vast domain, Qin Shi Huang Di was determined to finish what King Wuling had begun and bring the entire Yellow River loop under Chinese control.[22] In no time at all, General Meng Tian and his huge force managed to conquer the Ordos for the Qin empire and force its non-Chinese inhabitants to retreat to the northern side of the Yellow River. That accomplished, the First Emperor quickly adopted the old pattern established by Zhao and the other northern kingdoms of the Warring States period. He ordered the erection of long walls to protect his new territories from the nomadic peoples who had formerly inhabited them. According to the Records of the Grand Historian, Qin Shi Huang Di commanded his victorious general to build "walls along the [Yellow] river as frontier defenses," fortifications that historians believe incorporated much of King Wuling's old northern ramparts.[23] Thus was born what would eventually compose the northwesternmost segment of China's first great wall, the Great Wall of Qin Shi Huang Di.

QIN SHI HUANG DI AND THE THREAT FROM THE NORTH

After the fortifications north of the Yellow River loop were completed, Qin Shi Huang Di directed his top-ranking general to undertake a far more ambitious building project. According to Sima Qian, the First Sovereign Emperor commanded Meng Tian to erect a whole line of defenses extending from the beginning of the old state of Yan's frontier fortifications near the Bo Hai Gulf to the ramparts built by the former state of Qin in what is today the Chinese province of Gansu. Like the border ramparts of the Warring States period, Qin Shi Huang Di's wall was to come to a halt only where natural barriers such as sheer cliffs or narrow gullies could be relied on to keep out invading armies. According to Arthur Waldron, the emperor and his advisors considered their defensive wall building in the north as "a supplement to what nature had created," or as one early Chinese statesman put it, as a "way of providing boundaries where Heaven [the Supreme Deity] had neglected to make them clear."[24]

THE AMAZING TOMB OF QIN SHI HUANG DI

In 1974, a group of Chinese peasants digging a well near the site of the Qin dynasty's ancient capital at Xianyang in Shaanxi province made a remarkable discovery. They unearthed what is today considered as one of the world's greatest archaeological treasures: the gigantic underground tomb complex of China's First Sovereign Emperor, Qin Shi Huang Di. In three deep pits located about a mile to the east of the emperor's mausoleum, archaeologists have uncovered row after row of life-size terracotta figures of soldiers and horses. Amazingly, no two of the more than 7,000 meticulously detailed ceramic warriors have the exact same facial expression, hairstyle, or posture. Swords, crossbows, arrowheads, spears, and other actual weapons were also discovered in the pits, along with the imprints of numerous wooden chariots (which had long since rotted) and two beautifully wrought bronze chariots, each drawn by four bronze steeds.

Archaeologists have yet to excavate the main chamber of the First Emperor's tomb. In his Records of the Grand Historian, first-century B.C.. historian Sima Qian provides a tantalizing account of the tomb's lavish interior:

"From the time the First Emperor took the throne, work was begun on his mausoleum.... After he had won the empire, more than 700,000 conscripts from all parts of the country labored there. The laborers dug through three subterranean streams which they sealed off with bronze in order to make the burial chamber. This they filled with models of palaces, towers, and the hundred officials, as well as precious utensils, and marvelous rarities. Artisans were ordered to install mechanically triggered crossbows set to shoot any intruder. With mercury the various waterways of the empire, the Yangzi and Yellow Rivers, and even the

In carrying out his sovereign's orders to create a manmade boundary where no natural protective barriers such as high mountain ranges or wide rivers existed, Meng Tian would need to connect the existing ramparts of Yan, Zhao, and Qin with hundreds of miles of new construction. It was a mammoth undertaking, requiring the labor of many men and staggering sums of money to complete. As to why Qin Shi Huang Di felt

great ocean itself were created and made to flow and circulate mechanically. The heavenly constellations were depicted above and the geography of the earth was laid below. Lamps were fueled with whale oil so that they might burn forever without being extinguished.... Finally, trees and grass were planted on the mound to make it look like a mountain."*

*Quoted in Valerie Hansen, *The Open Empire: A History of China to 1600*, (New York: W.W. Norton, 2000), p.105.

In 1974, a group of Chinese peasants digging a well uncovered a giant tomb complex for the first Sovereign Emperor, Qin Shi Huang Di. They found more than 7,000 of these terracotta soldiers, no two of which are alike. The main chamber has yet to be excavated, but the site has become a major attraction for visitors to China.

compelled to invest such tremendous amounts of manpower and capital into creating an arbitrary line of earth and stone along virtually the entire length of the Chinese heartland's vast frontier with Inner Asia, historians cannot say with certainty.

"The classic reason" put forth by scholars for the creation of the first Great Wall is that the barrier was designed to keep nomadic raiders out of northern China's vulnerable farming villages.[25] "The reality," as Jonathan Fryer has observed, "was not quite so simple."[26] The sporadic nomadic raiding of border villages during the Warring States period continued to trouble northern China throughout Qin Shi Huang Di's reign. Nonetheless, as Fryer pointed out, it was not until after Qin Shi Huang Di's reign had ended that the scattered groups of Inner Asian nomads managed to organize themselves into a military federation capable of constituting a genuine threat to the Chinese Empire.

Some historians have sought an explanation for Qin Shi Huang Di's puzzling determination to erect a massive barrier between China and the as yet unorganized steppe nomads in the emperor's fearful and superstitious nature. Perhaps as a result of surviving three failed assassination attempts, over the course of his reign Qin Shi Huang Di became increasingly preoccupied with his own downfall and death. Obsessed with uncovering the secrets of immortality, he consulted scores of physicians, alchemists, and mystics, dispatched messengers to the farthest corners of his realm to obtain life-prolonging herbs and elixirs, and sponsored costly naval expeditions to fabled islands in the Yellow Sea where immortal beings were said to dwell. When the magical islands and potions could not be located, the emperor concluded that some evil being was thwarting his mission. To keep any malevolent spirits from spotting him as he went about his day-to-day business, he had his numerous palaces at Xianyang linked by walled, covered walkways. Qin Shi Huang Di even went so far as to order nearly one million laborers and craftsmen to secretly construct an elaborate underground tomb complex for him complete with 7,000 life-sized ceramic warriors to protect his soul from evil forces in the afterlife.

Some historians have suggested that the same deep-seated anxieties and superstitions that prompted Qin Shi Huang Di to build his huge mausoleum with its army of clay soldiers or launch lavish expeditions in quest of magical islands may also have spurred him to try to seal off his empire's northern frontiers with a gigantic wall. Ancient Chinese chronicles report that shortly before ordering the rampart's construction, the emperor received a cryptic note from a hermit and soothsayer who lived to the northeast of the Chinese heartland in Manchuria. "The one which will destroy Qin," the old Manchurian declared ominously, "is Hu."[27] "Hu" was a blanket term the ancient Chinese used to refer to the different groups of nomadic horsemen who inhabited Inner Asia's grassy plains. The emperor naturally concluded that the prophet's mysterious message meant his downfall would come at the hands of the Middle Kingdom's non-Chinese neighbors to the north. Given Qin Shi Huang Di's tendency toward paranoia and unquestioning faith in the supernatural, the old Manchurian's prophecy regarding the Hu was "probably one of the main factors" in his resolve to construct a huge defensive barrier between the Chinese heartland and the Inner Asian steppe even though the still unorganized nomads were incapable of inflicting serious damage on his kingdom.[28]

THE HUMAN COSTS OF BUILDING THE FIRST GREAT WALL

Historians can only speculate regarding the First Emperor's true motives and frame of mind when he ordered the creation of his "10,000-li" northern defense line. They have a much clearer conception of the horrific toll that the first Great Wall's construction took on Qin Shi Huang Di's downtrodden subjects.

According to Sima Qian in his Records of the Grand Historian, some 300,000 soldiers and 500,000 civilians toiled on the artificial boundary that Qin Shi Huang Di was determined to create between the Chinese people and their nomadic neighbors. Peasants, who composed the vast majority of China's population during Qin Shi Huang Di's reign (and throughout most of

Chinese history), made up the bulk of the Wall's half million-strong civilian work force. By order of the emperor, soldiers rounded up males from farming communities all over China and marched them off to the northern frontiers for months or even years at a stretch. As Qin Shi Huang Di had decreed that any male over the height of four feet could be drafted to build his border wall, even boys were compelled to leave their homes and families for long periods to help with the emperor's monstrous construction project. Women may also have been part of the wall's civilian work force. One ancient chronicler reported that Qin Shi Huang Di required the widows of men who had died while toiling on the northern rampart to labor in their late husbands' places.

Although most of the first Great Wall's civilian labor force consisted of law-abiding peasants, many convicted lawbreakers also toiled on the fortifications. Indeed, lawbreakers were plentiful in China during the Qin dynasty, and condemned criminals provided a vital source of labor not only for Qin Shi Huang Di's 10,000-li wall but also for the emperor's other ambitious building projects from his vast highway system to his magnificent mausoleum. The First Sovereign Emperor's enthusiasm for an ancient Chinese philosophy known as Legalism was closely linked to China's large criminal population. Legalism taught that humans are naturally evil and must be kept in check by a strict system of laws and punishments. Under the Legalist regime of Qin Shi Huang Di, a wide range of behaviors was deemed as wicked and deserving of criminal prosecution, not the least of which were speaking out against the emperor or trying to evade his compulsory labor service. Lawbreakers could expect to pay a heavy price for their crimes against society and the state. Those found guilty of even minor offenses faced deportation and confiscation of personal property. Those convicted of more serious crimes—including criticizing Qin Shi Huang Di or defying his edicts—could expect to be flogged, branded with hot irons, mutilated (most often by having the nose or one foot cut off), or executed. Death sentences were carried out by a variety of grisly

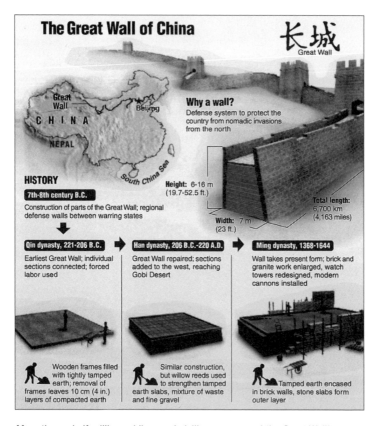

More than a half million soldiers and civilians composed the Great Wall's construction crew, and hundreds of thousands of these workers died due to the extreme physical demands of creating the wall. This diagram shows the history of the Wall's construction and various building techniques used.

methods, including cooking in a caldron of boiling water or live burial, as in the notorious case of the 460 Confucian scholars who refused to hand over their books. For many Chinese, however, the most dreaded punishment of all was beheading because decapitation "was thought to divide a person's head from the body even in the afterlife."[29]

Qin Shi Huang Di's subjects also had reason to dread a sentence handed down far more often by the First Emperor's draconian justice system than death by decapitation—four years hard labor on the empire's northern barricade. Indeed, the death toll among the builders of the first Great Wall was so high that the Chinese dubbed the immense barrier "The Longest Cemetery on Earth." Many workers died before even reaching the frontier, succumbing to exhaustion or dehydration during the grueling march from their home villages to China's northern fringes. Hundreds of thousands more died on the job or in the squalid, makeshift workers' camps that were hastily erected along the Great Wall's route.

The physical demands of fortifying the emperor's arbitrary border with the northern nomads were tremendous. Like the inter-kingdom and northern border walls of the Warring States period, most of the first Great Wall's new construction was carried out according to the arduous hang-tu method. Laborers slaved from dawn to dusk digging, dumping, and pounding earth as the barricade rose layer upon layer, four to six inches at a time. Using this excruciatingly slow and backbreaking technique, workers erected walls that are believed to have averaged 20 feet in height and 15–20 feet in width. At regular intervals along the rampart, laborers also constructed immense earthen signal and watchtowers, some soaring to 40 feet in height. Guards posted up and down the fortification lines communicated with one another from the towers by igniting fires after dark and sending smoke signals during daylight hours. As the emperor's new artificial boundary snaked across the rugged transition zone between the Chinese heartland and Inner Asia, workers had to build the Great Wall up hillsides and across vast plains and deserts, pressing on in searing heat and bitter cold, in rain and sleet and snow.

Chronic hunger added to the workers' misery. After Qin Shi Huang Di put Meng Tian in charge of overseeing the construction of his Great Wall, the general promptly set up a network of supply lines to get grain and vegetables from Chinese farming communities south of the northern frontier. Although Meng Tian stationed soldiers at regular intervals along the routes, the slow-moving supply carts made easy marks for roving gangs of bandits. Consequently, much of the food meant for the workers never made it to the Great Wall. According to one contemporary account, of the nearly 200 cartloads of grain sent northwestward from Shandong Peninsula to the barricade, just one arrived. The recurrent food shortages that plagued the first Great Wall's builders undoubtedly accelerated the already astronomical death toll as many laborers may have succumbed to malnutrition as well as to exhaustion, exposure, or disease. Chinese folklore says

THE SAD TALE OF MENG JIANGNU

A popular Chinese legend illustrates the suffering of the hundreds of thousands of Chinese fathers, sons, and husbands drafted to build the first Great Wall and the heartbreak of the loved ones they left behind. The tale of Meng Jiangnu tells of a young peasant woman from central China whose husband was dragged off by conscription officers one spring day to toil on the emperor's northern defenses. When autumn arrived and her beloved still had not returned home, Meng Jiangnu decided to travel to the border region to bring him warm clothing for the coming winter. After a long and difficult journey, Meng Jiangnu arrived at the Great Wall only to be informed that her husband had died from exhaustion. His remains, she was told, had been interred in the fortifications. The grieving widow's anguish was so great that her tears washed away 20 li of the earthen ramparts, revealing her husband's bones as well as those of his fallen comrades.

For many centuries, the Chinese believed that the corpses of the hundreds of thousands of workers who perished while slaving on the first Great Wall were buried within the ramparts. Recent archaeological research, however, has confirmed what historians had long suspected: deceased laborers were buried in ditches near the ramparts and not within the wall itself. Scholars realized that if bodies had been interred in the Wall, the structure could not have survived. The decomposing corpses would have made the wall unstable by causing air pockets to form within its earthen layers.

that one worker perished for every meter (approximately one yard) of the Qin Wall.

THE END OF THE QIN DYNASTY

In 210 B.C., Qin Shi Huang Di died suddenly at the age of 49. Ironically, at the time of his death, the emperor was on a journey to eastern China to confer with an alchemist who had supposedly developed an immortality elixir. Although Qin Shi Huang Di's death remains shrouded in mystery, some historians speculate that he may have succumbed to mercury poisoning since mercury was a common ingredient in the elixirs and drugs of ancient China.

With the emperor's demise, the dynasty he had founded began to disintegrate almost immediately. Revolts broke out in central China and soon spread across the empire as the Chinese people rose up against the brutal laws and tyrannical policies of the Qin regime. The strongest opposition to the dynasty came from the peasant masses compelled to slave on Qin Shi Huang Di's ambitious building projects, including his huge defensive wall in the north. Just as the burden of the First Emperor's ruthless conscription policies fell hardest on those at the bottom of Chinese society, so too did the crippling weight of the taxes he imposed to pay for his enormous northern barrier as well as his elaborate underground tomb complex, vast highway system, and lavish palaces.

Although the autocratic Qin Shi Huang Di had managed to keep a lid on popular dissatisfaction throughout his 11-year reign, his young and inexperienced successors, the Second Emperor (who died under mysterious circumstances in 206 B.C.) and the Third Emperor could do little to quell the peasant uprisings that erupted after their father's death. Within four years of the First Sovereign Emperor's demise, the dynasty that Qin Shi Huang Di had once boasted would last for 10,000 generations officially ended with the execution of the Third Emperor by rebel forces.

Shortly after the death of the Third Emperor in 206 B.C., one of the rebel leaders, a commoner named Liu Bang, boldly proclaimed himself as China's new ruler. Four years later, Liu Bang assumed the title of Gao Zu, emperor of the Middle Kingdom and "High Progenitor" (patriarch) of a new dynasty, the Han.

In the meantime, an important transformation was taking place to the north of the Chinese heartland in the grassy plains of Inner Asia. Scattered bands of nomadic horsemen were starting to unite under the leadership of a fierce tribe known as the Xiongnu. For the first time, the Middle Kingdom was confronted by a powerful political and military confederation of Inner Asians—what one historian has dubbed "the earliest steppe empire in world history."[30] The warlike Xiongnu would pose a significant threat to the new Han dynasty, a challenge that its leaders would attempt to meet in a variety of ways, not the least of which would be strengthening—and dramatically extending—the arbitrary boundary of stone and earth created by Qin Shi Huang Di between the Chinese and their nomadic neighbors to the north.

4

The Great Wall
of the Han
Dynasty

During Gao Zu's reign, the internal strife and bloodshed that had plagued China ever since Qin Shi Huang Di's death continued. Quelling the uprisings that erupted on a regular basis throughout his sprawling kingdom consumed much of the first Han ruler's time and energy. In contrast to the final years of the Qin dynasty, power-hungry nobles and not disgruntled peasants were the driving force behind most of the rebellions. Determined to retain the loyalty of the ordinary men and women who had helped bring him to power, Gao Zu took to heart a traditional Chinese saying: "The prince is the boat; the common people are the water. The water can support the boat, or the water can capsize the boat."[31] Accordingly, although Gao Zu kept the strong centralized government of his predecessors, he lowered taxes and made punishments less harsh than under the Qin. Moreover, he released China's vast peasantry from the onerous labor duties of the Qin years, abandoning all construction on the Great Wall and on Qin Shi Huang Di's other mammoth building projects.

THE RISE OF THE XIONGNU CONFEDERATION

With the bulk of his financial and military resources devoted to suppressing internal challenges to his rule from the nobility, Gao Zu neglected the great northern defense system created by Qin Shi Huang Di. Heavily patrolled during Qin Shi Huang Di's reign, the first Great Wall was now left virtually unmanned. Ironically, during the First Sovereign Emperor's reign, no expense had been spared to strengthen and garrison the northern fortifications even though the danger presented by the divided steppe nomads remained minimal. Now the defense system was being abandoned by Gao Zu at the very moment that the Middle Kingdom faced an unprecedented military challenge from the grasslands of Inner Asia: the powerful Xiongnu confederation. Little is known with certainty regarding the ethnic background or language of these warlike people who led Inner Asia's first steppe empire. Some scholars believe that the Xiongnu were related to the Turks; others have linked them to the Mongols. According to conventional wisdom, the Xiongnu were the eastern branch of the famous Huns who overran the Roman Empire in the fifth century A.D.

Under the skillful guidance of their youthful new chieftain or shanyu, Mo-tun (reigned 209–174 B.C.), the Xiongnu began to achieve dominance in Inner Asia during the last years of the Qin dynasty. Remarkably driven and utterly ruthless, Mo-tun allegedly became supreme leader of the Xiongnu after murdering his own father, the former shanyu. Once in power, Mo-tun lost no time in exploiting China's political instability to increase his tribe's territory and influence. The Xiongnu were among the nomadic groups expelled from the Ordos by General Meng Tian early in Qin Shi Huang Di's reign, and Mo-tun was determined to reclaim the area's vast grazing grounds for his followers. With the imperial army busy quashing the popular revolts that followed Qin Shi Huang Di's death in 210 B.C., Mo-tun's forces had little trouble pushing southward through the gates of the Great Wall and laying claim to the lands within the Yellow River's large northwestern bend.

Mo-tun also turned his attention to the Xiongnu's neighboring tribes in Inner Asia. One by one, Mo-tun and his warriors subjugated or drove out rival nomadic groups. Soon the Xiongnu had become the undisputed rulers of a vast empire centered in what is today the Inner Mongolian Autonomous Region and including most of the modern Mongolian Republic and Xinjiang Uighur Autonomous Region.

BRIBES AND BRIDES: THE HE QIN POLICY

By 202 B.C., when Gao Zu officially founded the Han dynasty, the far-flung tribal confederacy led by Mo-tun had become a major thorn in China's side. Determined to tap the Middle Kingdom's wealth, large armies of mounted Xiongnu archers crossed the arbitrary border between the nomads and Chinese established by Qin Shi Huang Di and tyrannized the empire's northern frontiers. Nomadic raiding of Chinese towns was not only more violent than ever before but more widespread as Mo-tun led his warriors in attacks against communities farther and farther south of the now unmanned Great Wall.

Resolved to teach China's troublesome neighbors a lesson, in 200 B.C., Gao Zu led a large military expedition to his empire's northern fringes to confront the Xiongnu. As it turned out, he and his advisors had gravely underestimated the size of Mo-tun's forces as well as their formidable riding and shooting skills. "With their bows and bone-tipped arrows," Arthur Waldron observed, the fast-riding Xiongnu "could lay down a barrage 'like rain,' an image used in both Chinese and western sources."[32] In no time, Mo-tun's army had managed to trap Gao Zu and his men in a walled city, cutting them off from all supplies and reinforcements.

In return for his freedom, Gao Zu signed a peace treaty with Mo-tun that included a number of humiliating provisions. The emperor agreed to give the shanyu substantial quantities of millet, wine, and silk cloth, which the Xiongnu prized for its sheer texture and rich colors, and a Chinese princess to be his wife. Thus began what would come to be known in China as the *he qin* (harmonious kinship) policy. This appeasement-minded strategy of trying to pacify the Xiongnu through expensive gifts and royal marriages would dominate Chinese relations with Inner Asia's first steppe empire for the next seven decades. Han emperors pledged to maintain formal diplomatic relations with the Xiongnu as a co-equal or "brotherly" state, make large yearly offerings of grain, silk, gold, and other goods to the shanyu, and promote kinship ties between the two empires through giving Chinese princesses to nomad chieftains in marriage. Royal marriages were an important feature of the he qin agreements. For the nomads, intermarriage with the Chinese royalty entailed more than establishing court-to-court blood ties; it also "meant dowries, wedding gifts, and more ready access to the Chinese marketplace," as the authors of a recent study on nomad–Chinese relations observe.[33] In return for the Chinese brides and bribes, the Xiongnu's supreme leader pledged to stop sending his warriors into the Chinese heartland.

The he qin policy was designed to dissuade the Xiongnu's leaders from invading and plundering the Middle Kingdom by guaranteeing them regular subsidies of valuable Chinese goods. To ensure that ordinary Xiongnu could readily obtain Chinese products by other means than looting, the Han emperors opened a number of government-regulated frontier markets. Eager to secure those agricultural and manufactured goods that they could not easily produce for themselves because of their mobile lifestyle, Xiongnu herdsmen thronged to the new trading stations, most of which were located along Qin Shi Huang Di's Great Wall. At the border markets, the nomads offered hides, fur, wool, and live-stock—particularly their horses, which despite their compact size were renowned for their vigor and swiftness—in exchange for Chinese grains, metal and ceramic utensils, and cloth.

CHINESE DISSATISFACTION WITH THE HE QIN POLICY

As the Han rulers soon discovered, not all of China's northern neighbors were willing to give up raiding for trading. Despite the establishment of the new frontier markets and their chieftain's prohibition against attacking China, bands of renegade Xiongnu horsemen continued to loot the Middle Kingdom's northern provinces throughout the reigns of Gao Zu and his son Wen Di (reigned 179–157 B.C.) and grandson Jing Di (reigned 157–141 B.C.). On several occasions, large nomad raiding parties actually came within sight of the Han capital at Chang-an (the present-day city of Xi'an in Shanxi province).

Wen Di became so frustrated by the raiding that he even contemplated launching a military offensive against the Xiongnu, despite his father's nearly disastrous experience with Mo-tun's forces in 200 B.C. He abandoned his invasion plan only after consulting with his Minister of War, who strongly cautioned the emperor against trying to confront the fast-riding, battle-hardened Xiongnu on their own turf, saying:

> The Hsiung-nu [Xiongnu] scale and descend even the most precipitous mountains with astonishing speed. They swim

the deepest torrents, tolerate wind and rain, hunger and thirst. They can set off on forced marches unhindered even by precipices. They train their horses to cope with the narrowest trails, and are so expert with their bows that in a surprise attack they can fire their arrows at full gallop.... They attack, recoil and rally again, and if ever they do suffer a setback they simply disappear without a trace like a cloud.[34]

Although the early Han emperors and their advisors rejected a military solution to the ongoing Xiongnu problem as too risky, many leading government officials and intellectuals were extremely uncomfortable with the he qin approach of trying to control the nomads peacefully. Convinced that Xiongnu culture was vastly inferior to their own, they were appalled by their rulers' willingness to flatter the shanyu and buy him off with costly gifts, princesses, and "brotherly" diplomatic relations, particularly in the face of continued nomadic raiding of China.

Official Han documents tactfully portrayed the Xiongnu as the equals of the Chinese. In truth, however, many statesmen and scholars scorned their northern neighbors as barbarians. This attitude of cultural and moral superiority toward the Xiongnu is reflected in the writings of the influential historian of the Han period, Sima Qian. In stark contrast to the Chinese, the Xiongnu lacked both a well-developed code of morality and a written language—even their "laws are only verbal," Sima Qian noted in his Records of the Grand Historian.[35] Moreover, he observed, the Xiongnu "have no walled cities or fixed residences, nor any agricultural activities."[36] As far as the Han historian could tell, all that the nomads excelled at was warfare and plunder. Their inborn greed, he declared, spurred the Xiongnu to terrorize and pillage their settled neighbors without the slightest hesitation. "The reason that they carry out robbing and looting is because their nature is so," Sima Qian wrote, adding, "When they see the enemy, eager for booty, they swoop down like a flock of birds."[37] On the battlefield, the self-seeking Xiongnu displayed not a trace of the Chinese soldier's deep sense of honor and duty, Sima Qian asserted. Xiongnu warriors, he remarked disdainfully, "do not regard running away [from battle] as something shameful; they only care about li [profit] and do not know of ... yi [righteousness]."[38]

The dismay with which many Chinese officials and intellectuals viewed the he qin strategy is also evident in a much-quoted memorial to Wen Di by the statesman and poet, Jia Yi. According to Jia Yi, the entire natural order was upset when the Chinese sovereign made offerings to the shanyu. The he qin policy, he proclaimed, was "a source of shame for those who are in charge of the affairs of the empire" because the strategy made a mockery of the kingdom's Heaven-appointed hierarchy:

> The situation of the empire may be described as like that of a person hanging upside down. The Son of Heaven [the traditional title for the Chinese ruler, the supposed intermediary between humankind and Heaven] is the head of the empire. Why? Because he should remain on the top. The barbarians are the feet of the empire. Why? Because they should be placed at the bottom. Now, the Hsiung-nu [Xiongnu] are arrogant and insolent on the one hand, and invade and plunder us on the other hand, which must be considered as an expression of extreme disrespect toward us.... Yet each year Han provides them with money, silk floss [thread] and fabrics. To command the barbarian is the power vested in the Emperor on the top, and to present tribute to the Son of Heaven is a ritual to be performed by the vassals at the bottom. Hanging upside down like this is something beyond comprehension.[39]

Although Jia Yi and the he qin policy's other critics maintained that the "uncivilized" shanyu should meekly submit to his Chinese superiors instead of arrogantly demanding costly gifts from them, they failed to offer suggestions as to just how this major shift in the empire's foreign relations might be accomplished. Consequently, for lack of a better alternative, the he qin strategy continued to hold sway in China for another quarter of a century after Jia Yi's death. Only during the reign of Wen Di's dynamic and confident grandson, Wu Di, did the Middle Kingdom adopt a more assertive strategy for dealing with the Xiongnu, a strategy in which the long-neglected northern defense line of Qin Shi Huang Di would play an important part.

THE MARTIAL EMPEROR TAKES ON THE XIONGNU

Probably the most celebrated ruler in the 400-year history of the Han dynasty, was Wu Di—"the Martial [warlike] Emperor." Wu Di assumed the throne in 141 B.C. and governed China for the next 54 years until his death in 87 B.C. Determined to take a more aggressive stance toward the Xiongnu than his predecessors, during the first years of his reign, the young emperor focused much of his considerable energies on strengthening and updating the Chinese military.

Although Chinese cavalry units had existed since the Warring States period, throughout the Qin and early Han dynasties, the imperial army continued to rely heavily on its relatively slow-moving infantry and charioteers in battle. To compete effectively with the more mobile Xiongnu horsemen, Wu Di realized, China needed to place new emphasis on its mounted forces. Accordingly, he significantly expanded the imperial cavalry while at the same time subsidizing dozens of horse breeding stations on the Middle Kingdom's Inner Asian frontiers to ensure his highly trained troops a steady supply of fresh mounts. To further bolster China's fighting power, Wu Di equipped the imperial forces with the latest weaponry, including the recently developed "multiple-shooting or 'repetition' crossbows," the first crossbow in Chinese history that was "superior to the nomadic bow" in battle.[40]

Less than a decade after ascending the throne, the Martial Emperor decided that his new and improved army was ready to challenge the Xiongnu on their own turf. In 133 B.C., he sent 300,000 troops deep into the heart of Xiongnu country. Chinese armies even penetrated as far as northern Korea where Wu Di established four commanderies in order to "flank the Xiongnu

on their eastern border."[41] After more than two decades of inter-
mittent fighting and the loss of tens of thousands of men and
many more horses, Wu Di finally managed to push the Xiongnu
out of the pasturelands closest to the Chinese heartland and
north of the arbitrary boundary between nomad and Chinese
defined by Qin Shi Huang Di's Great Wall.

WU DI REDISCOVERS THE GREAT WALL

Once the Xiongnu had been driven out of all the territory to
the south of the Qin Great Wall, including the strategic Yellow
River loop or Ordos region, Wu Di turned his attention to
securing China's frontiers against any future threats from the
Inner Asian steppes. The massive northern defense system of
Qin Shi Huang Di, he decided, must be repaired and re-gar-
risoned along its entire length.

The considerable expense and difficulties involved in transporting food northward to the Great Wall had discouraged Wu
Di's Han predecessors from posting large defensive forces along
China's borders with the Xiongnu. Supplies could not be easily
conveyed northward by water, because "the Yellow River and
other natural water routes ran downhill to the China plain, so
that barges carrying men or material had to go against the cur-
rent."[42] Transporting grain and other foodstuffs overland to the
frontiers was both risky and costly. As in Qin Shi Huang Di's day,
gangs of bandits often preyed on the slow-moving supply carts
as they made their way to the remote barricade. Intent on avoid-
ing the problems associated with transporting food northward
to the frontier, the Martial Emperor devised a more cost-effective and reliable way of feeding the wall's garrisons. *Tuntian*
(military farms) were created along the ramparts, where troops
could grow their own millet, barley, and other food crops and
thus be self-supporting.

During Wu Di's reign, "military efficiency was brought to a
high standard on the Great Wall."[43] Most of the soldiers dispatched to the Great Wall worked and lived in one of its numerous watchtowers. Although their chief responsibility was

keeping a sharp eye out for any suspicious enemy movements and taking defensive action if necessary, the watchtower units also manufactured arrows, maintained detailed inventories of supplies and weapons, and exchanged signals using smoke, flags, or torches with other garrisons up and down the rampart on a "precisely timed schedule as well as in emergency."[44] Other border troops were responsible for raising food crops on the government-sponsored tuntian, transporting official reports and correspondence on horseback among the fortification's various command posts according to a carefully designed relay system, and keeping the wall and its towers, forts, and other structures in good repair.

WU DI LOOKS WESTWARD

Wu Di did more than merely restore and re-garrison the Qin Great Wall. In the Chinese Empire's second major campaign of wall building, Wu Di also extended Qin Shi Huang Di's fortifications for several hundred miles into the arid wilderness that lay to the west of the Chinese heartland. By doing so, the Martial Emperor created a new arbitrary border for China in the northwest, one that cut directly through desert regions that had traditionally been the realm of the Xiongnu and other nomadic tribes.

Wu Di's decision to extend the Qin Great Wall—and China's borders—to the west, had its roots in the early years of his reign when he sent his trusted commander, General Zhang Qian, to Central Asia on a diplomatic mission. Zhang's assignment was to forge a military alliance against the Xiongnu with the large Yuezhi tribe, which had been driven westward by Mo-tun's forces from modern-day Gansu province years earlier. After many misfortunes and delays, the general finally hunted down the elusive Yuezhi in Bactria (modern northern Afghanistan), only to discover that they had no interest in returning east to fight their old enemy the Xiongnu.

Zhang Qian's western expedition may have been a diplomatic failure, but Wu Di was thrilled by the wealth of information he brought back about India, Parthia (present-day Iran), Ferghana (in modern Uzbekistan), and the other rich and sophisticated civilizations he had visited or heard about during the course of

SILK: CHINA'S MOST PRIZED EXPORT

The most highly valued Chinese product to be transported along the Silk Road was the commodity for which the famous trade route was named. Soft, sheer, and lightweight, silk symbolized wealth and high social status and typically sold for exorbitant prices in the West, particularly in Rome where silk garments were all the rage among the upper classes. (Despite the huge popularity of Chinese silk in Rome, the Chinese remained unaware of that great empire's existence because all transactions with Roman textile merchants were conducted through Parthian and Indian middlemen.)

The ancient Chinese were able to monopolize the lucrative silk trade because from about the mid-third century B.C. to the mid-sixth century A.D., they alone understood the long and meticulous process of making silk from the cocoons of the silkworm (a kind of caterpillar). To coax them into making their cocoons, Chinese silk manufacturers coddled the silkworms day and night. From the moment they hatched, the caterpillars were kept at strictly monitored temperatures and fed the tender leaves of the mulberry tree at precisely timed intervals. When the fully grown silkworms had finally spun their precious cocoons, workers boiled the cocoons, reeled off (unwound) their long filaments of silk, and then patiently twisted a number of the thin stands together to produce thicker and stronger threads. The thread was then dyed a range of brilliant colors and woven on looms into a delicate yet remarkably resilient fabric.

According to legend, the Middle Kingdom lost its long monopoly over silk production when a Chinese woman engaged to marry a Central Asian prince secretly transported a silk cocoon out of the empire in her long hair. Historians, however, believe that the secrets of silk production were actually carried to the West about A.D. 550 by two spies working for the Byzantine (Eastern Roman) emperor, Justinian I. Nonetheless, even after Byzantium, Persia (modern-day Iran), and India began producing their own silk, "the Chinese retained a competitive edge because their superior technology produced more densely woven silks with more complex weaves."*

*Quoted in Valerie Hansen, *The Open Empire: A History of China to 1600*, (New York: W.W. Norton, 2000), p.174.

his wanderings. The emperor was particularly interested in Zhang's accounts of the bustling east–west trade routes that linked Central Asia with Parthia, Syria, and other kingdoms in what is today called the Middle East.

Wu Di resolved to carve out a role for China in these lucrative commercial networks, especially after Zhang informed him that Chinese silk had somehow traveled westward—probably along unknown tribal trading paths—to Ferghana and Parthia where it was greatly prized by those kingdom's wealthiest citizens. Soon, caravans laden with ceramics, spices, and, above all, silk thread and fabric, began wending their way westward from the Chinese heartland through today's Gansu province. On the eastern fringes of the Takla Makan Desert in the modern region of Xinjiang, the caravans took one of two separate routes that skirted that vast and forbidding wasteland to the oasis town of Kashgar (on Xinjiang's western border). From Kashgar most of the Chinese goods were first transported to India or Parthia, and from there, as far west as Rome. Eventually, this complex of trade routes connecting China with Central Asia, the Middle East, and the Roman Empire would come to be known as the Silk Road, after China's most sought-after export.

A NEW USE FOR THE GREAT WALL: PROTECTING CHINESE TRADE

Although Wu Di was delighted with China's lucrative new commercial ventures, they brought fresh problems for the emperor to tackle. It did not take long for bandits—including fast-riding nomadic raiders from the Inner Asian steppes—to hear of the costly goods traveling out of China beyond the western fringes of the Great Wall. To Wu Di's dismay, plundering of silk-laden caravans traveling out of China, as well as of merchant convoys journeying to the Middle Kingdom with horses, jade, glass, and other valuable foreign commodities, had became commonplace by the end of the second century B.C.

Resolved to safeguard China's profitable new international trade, Wu Di ordered that the great barricade built by Qin Shi Huang Di be extended westward from its old terminus (end

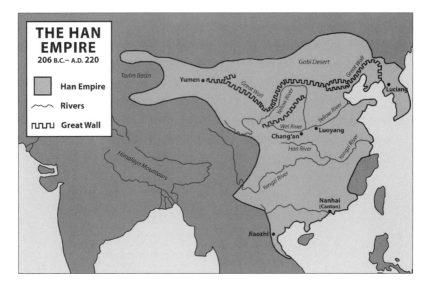

During the Han Dynasty, emperor Wu Di restored the Great Wall and also extended it several miles into the western wilderness. This map shows China and the location of the Great Wall within the Han Empire.

point) at Lintao in central Gansu province. The addition was to stretch more than 300 miles northwest from Lintao all the way through the narrow Gansu (or Hexi) Corridor to Xinjiang's Lop Nor Desert, which borders the Takla Makan Desert on the east and north.

Building the Great Wall's new branch in the arid lands of western Gansu and Xinjiang was a formidable task. Hundreds of thousands of soldiers, peasant conscripts, and convicted criminals braved the searing summer heat and brutal winter cold of China's far northwest to fashion the fortifications according to the slow and laborious hang-tu method. In the absence of other building materials, the new defenses were constructed from moistened sand and gravel layered with willow reeds and branches from the tamarisk, a desert shrub. By Wu Di's orders, a chain of massive watchtowers, some 30 feet tall, were also erected along the wall within sight of one another.

To safeguard the Chinese and foreign caravans entering and leaving the Middle Kingdom through Xinjiang and the Gansu

Corridor, Wu Di stationed large garrisons along his imposing new western defense line. In addition to providing excellent protection to merchants traversing the Silk Road, the emperor's heavily manned extension of the Great Wall also provided an incentive to colonize nearby lands. The Han government resettled thousands of Chinese citizens along the empire's arbitrary new borderline in the northwest. Many of the colonists struggled

BUDDHISM COMES TO CHINA ALONG THE SILK ROAD

Not only material goods but also ideas were carried into China along the East–West trade routes that the Great Wall helped to safeguard during the days of the Han dynasty. Without a doubt, the most influential of these intellectual imports to the Middle Kingdom was Buddhism. Buddhism, which was destined to have a profound impact on Chinese thought and culture, is believed to have first reached China's northwestern trading centers from India during the early second century A.D.

Based on the teachings of a sixth-century B.C. Indian prince known as the Buddha (meaning the enlightened one), Buddhism's first "Noble Truth" or principle was that life is suffering. The cause of all life's suffering, according to the Buddha, was worldly desires. By following the Buddha's ethical rules and renouncing all worldly cravings, ambitions, and attachments, believers could eventually be freed from life's miseries, including fear, pain, and even death, and attain Nirvana, an eternal state of enlightenment and bliss.

After its introduction, Buddhism spread rapidly from the fortified town of Dunhuang and other trading centers along the far western section of the Great Wall to the empire's heartland, attracting followers from among all of China's various economic and social classes. Buddhism met the emotional and spiritual needs of the Chinese in ways that traditional Chinese religions and philosophies, including Confucianism, could not: "It appealed to people in China above all because it addressed questions of suffering and death with a directness unmatched in native Chinese traditions. It offered a fully developed vision of the afterlife and the prospect of salvation, promising that all creatures might one day find blissful release from suffering."*

*Quoted in Patricia Buckley Ebrey, *The Cambridge Illustrated History of China* (Cambridge: Cambridge University Press, 1996), p. 97.

to coax crops out of the region's arid soil to supply food to the Great Wall's western garrisons as well as to merchants and other travelers passing through. Others flocked to the bustling new trading centers like the highly fortified town of Dunhuang, which were built along the gates of the wall's western extension. At the new commercial centers, traders from far-off lands exchanged goods as well as ideas with the Chinese. It was by means of the Silk Road that Buddhism, the religion that was destined to become China's third great faith along with Confucianism and Daoism, made its way into the Middle Kingdom from India around the early second century A.D.

Throughout history, the creators of artificial boundaries between peoples or nations have typically sought to closely monitor their arbitrary borders. The arbitrary border established by Wu Di in present-day Gansu and Xinjiang was no exception to this rule. The Han government strictly controlled all comings and goings at the western Great Wall's busy gates. Acting much like modern-day customs agents, soldiers posted at the heavily fortified portals scrutinized the papers of merchants and other travelers wishing to enter the Chinese Empire. Anyone requesting to leave the country was closely questioned in order to keep army deserters, traitors, or criminals from escaping into the remote desert regions beyond China's new western boundaries. In addition, the guards stationed at the wall's gates were responsible for carefully examining all goods heading in or out of the empire to prevent the smuggling of weapons and other contraband.

THE END OF THE HAN DYNASTY AND ITS WESTERN WALL

For two centuries after Wu Di's death in 87 B.C., the heavily manned northwestern branch of the Great Wall continued to play a vital role in protecting and overseeing China's flourishing trade with the countries along the Silk Road. During the late second and early third centuries A.D., as the Han dynasty weakened in the face of administrative incompetence, bitter court rivalries, and popular uprisings, the beleaguered government could no longer maintain its military outposts or political sway in the remote northwest, however. The garrisons in western Gansu and in Xinjiang were recalled and the ramparts fell into disrepair as China's northwestern boundaries contracted to their pre-Wu Di position. Over the centuries following the official end of Han rule in A.D. 220, more and more of the western fortifications were buried under drifting sand. In time, the Han branch of the Great Wall would be forgotten altogether. Not until the early twentieth century would the barricade's windswept ruins be rediscovered by archaeologists.

With the collapse of the Han dynasty, China descended into the aptly named Period of Disunity (A.D. 220–589) during which the empire fragmented into a host of rival kingdoms and suffered repeated invasions by Inner Asian tribes. During this tumultuous era, a succession of short-lived, non-Chinese ruling houses held sway over northern China. Ironically, in hopes of safeguarding their new domains from incursions by rival Inner Asian groups, several of these tribal dynasties would repair and extend the Great Wall—the same arbitrary boundary of earth and stone that China's First Sovereign Emperor had created to keep nomadic "barbarians" such as themselves out of the Chinese heartland in the first place.

5

From the Period of Disunity Through the Mongol Conquest: The Great Wall in War and Peace

From the third century A.D. until the empire was finally reunited in the sixth century, southern China was governed by six successive Chinese dynasties centered in the Yangzi Valley while a series of short-lived Inner Asian dynasties controlled parts or all of northern China. China's chief threat from the Inner Asian steppe was no longer the Xiongnu, whose once vast federation had completely disintegrated by the end of the Han dynasty. Now the principal menace to northern China was a nomadic alliance led by the Tuoba (Toba), a powerful clan within the warlike Xian Bei tribe. Sometime after the fall of the Han dynasty, the Tuoba migrated southward from Inner Mongolia through the neglected fortifications of the Great Wall to occupy territory in what is today's northern Shanxi province. By 386, the Tuoba alliance had expanded its control over all of northern China and founded what would prove to be one of the longest lasting Inner Asian dynasties of the turbulent Period of Disunity (220–589), the Northern Wei.

THE NORTHERN WEI ADOPT WALL BUILDING AND OTHER CHINESE WAYS

Northern China's new rulers did not attempt to impose their own nomadic culture and economic system on the people they had overrun. Instead, the Tuoba leadership ordered their tribes to abandon full-time herding for farming, insisting that they settle and till the soil alongside the Chinese. The Northern Wei court also enthusiastically adopted Chinese ways, taking Chinese surnames, using Chinese script for writing, wearing Chinese-style clothing, and even appointing veteran Chinese bureaucrats as government officials. According to Patricia Buckley Ebrey, "It was expedient for [the Tuoba] to employ Chinese officials and adopt the institutions they proposed, because the total number of Xian Bei and other northern tribesmen in their confederacy could not have been more than a couple of million, but the Chinese, over whom they were trying to maintain military control, numbered twenty or thirty million or more."[45]

As the Tuoba embraced Chinese ways and came to rely more and more on settled agriculture, they soon confronted the same problems with nomadic raiding that had troubled their Chinese predecessors. To protect their new domain from the large raiding parties of the ferocious Ruanruan tribe that had settled in Inner Mongolia after the Xian Bei migrated southward, the Northern Wei leaders, with their deep respect for all things Chinese, naturally turned their attention to the Great Wall. In 432, the Tuoba emperor drafted thousands of peasant laborers to rebuild 600 miles of Qin Shi Huang Di's crumbling earthen defense line from today's Shanxi province eastward to Hebei province. His successors continued the restoration work and even constructed an entirely new branch of the wall encircling the Northern Wei capital of Pingcheng (present-day Datong in northern Shanxi).

According to Arthur Waldron, one of the most "thorough and complete expositions of the virtues of wall-building" in Chinese history was written not by a Chinese statesman but rather by a Northern Wei official named Gao Lu.[46] Although delivered to a court "whose origins were nomadic," Gao Lu's memorial, "In Favor of Long Walls," contrasted the "strengths and weaknesses of settled and steppe peoples in words that show not a trace of nomadic influence."[47] Defensive wall-building, Gao Lu declared, was the best approach to controlling the Ruanruan and other "barbarians" because the northerners were:

> fierce and simple-minded, like wild birds or beasts. Their strength is fighting in the open fields; their weakness is in attacking fortified places. If we take advantage of the weakness of the northern barbarians, and thereby overcome their strength, then even if they are very numerous, they will not become a disaster for us, and even if they arrive, they will not be able to penetrate our territory.[48]

The minister concluded his memorial by summarizing the "five advantages of long walls," advantages that would be cited time and time again by future supporters of defensive border walls, particularly during the Ming dynasty (1368–1644) when wall building would reach its apex in the Middle Kingdom:

> We calculate that building long walls has five advantages. First, it eliminates the problems of mobile defense. Second, it permits the northern tribes to nomadize [beyond the wall] and thus eliminates the disasters of raiding. Third, because it enables us to look for the enemy from the top of the wall, it means we no longer wait [to be attacked, not knowing where the enemy is]. Fourth, it removes anxiety about border defense, and the need to mount defense when it is not necessary. And fifth, it permits the easy transport of supplies, and therefore prevents insufficiency.[49]

WALL BUILDING PICKS UP MOMENTUM UNDER THE NORTHERN QI AND SUI DYNASTIES

In 535, the Northern Wei empire collapsed following a mutiny by Xian Bei garrisons along the northern frontier. The rebellious soldiers viewed the Tuoba leadership's growing emphasis on static defense (in other words, wall building) over offensive campaigns as a sign of weakness and resented the high-living court's fondness for costly Chinese luxuries. In time, two rival Xian Bei kingdoms would emerge from the wreckage of the old Northern Wei empire: the Northern Qi in northeastern China and the Northern Zhou in northwestern China.

Soon after establishing their dynasty in 550, the leaders of the Northern Qi, the more "Chinese" in outlook and customs of the Wei's two successors, resumed wall building with a passion. According to one source, the Northern Qi drafted nearly 2 million peasant laborers to rebuild and extend the Great Wall along the arbitrary borders they had established on the western and northern fringes of their new domain. These defense lines were intended to provide protection against both the Northern Zhou and nomadic invaders from the steppes. In all, the wall segments restored or added by the Northern Qi during their 27-year-long reign totaled nearly 1,000 miles, making the Qi the most enthu-siastic wall builders since Qin Shi Huang Di.

Of all the various nomadic groups against which the Northern Qi sought to fortify their borders, the one that most alarmed them was the Turkish-speaking Tujue. The Tujue, who had conquered the Northern Wei's old enemy, the Ruanruan, were rapidly becoming the rulers of a steppe empire that stretched from Manchuria to Afghanistan and included most of the Ordos region of the Yellow River's loop. Even after splitting into eastern and western branches in 582, the Tujue empire remained a formidable threat to the Qi and Zhou dynasties' strong new successor in northern China after 581, the Sui. Established by a fiercely ambitious Zhou general of mixed Chinese and Xian Bei heritage, by 589, the Sui dynasty not only controlled most of northern China but all of the southern Middle Kingdom as well, making it the first ruling house to pre-side over a united China in more than three centuries.

Profoundly concerned about the growing Turkish menace in the steppes and deserts to the Chinese heartland's north and west, the Sui founder, Emperor Wen resumed work on the Great Wall almost immediately after taking power. In 585, he sent 30,000 men to the Ordos to construct a new branch of the wall that cut diagonally across the territory enclosed by the Yellow River's bend. Getting as much territory as possible inside China's newest arbitrary border with its nomadic rivals was clearly not of paramount importance to Emperor Wen. Convinced that China lacked the military might to dislodge the Tujue com-pletely from the Ordos, the emperor erected his defensive ram-parts many miles to the south of Qin Shi Huang Di's old boundary on the northern side of the Yellow River's big arch.

As Jonathan Fryer has noted, Wen Di's son and successor, Yang Di, strongly believed "that it was best to follow a policy of 'walking on two feet,' when dealing with the barbarians ... in other words, to have two policies side by side, the first to wall them off and the second to maintain good relations with the tribes on the other side of the protective screen."[50] Although

Yang Di was willing to try almost anything to placate the Tujue, from offering them the traditional brides and bribes of the Han dynasty's old he qin policy to journeying to the steppes to pay his personal respects to their chieftain, he was nonetheless a zealous wall builder. In 607, for example, Yang Di conscripted one million peasants to build an extension of the Great Wall to the southeast of the Yellow River loop in just 10 days. The emperor's giant labor force completed the construction on time but at a shocking cost. According to one account, only half of the workers survived.

While he was compelling huge work gangs to renovate and extend the Great Wall at a breakneck pace, Yang Di was also drafting millions of peasants to slave on the construction project for which he is best remembered—the Grand Canal. Designed to link China's chief rivers, the Yellow River in the north and the Yangzi in the south, this 1,200-mile-long network of canals is widely considered one of the greatest engineering feats of its time in the world. Sometimes referred to as an artificial Nile River, the Grand Canal enabled rice and other foodstuffs from the highly productive lands of the south to be transported north and created a foundation for a unified national economy in the sprawling Chinese Empire.

In 1612, Yang Di launched a series of ambitious military campaigns beyond the traditional northeastern boundaries of the Chinese Empire to modern Korea. According to historian J.A.G. Roberts, the campaigns were prompted by Yang Di's concerns regarding a possible alliance between the Koreans and China's old enemy, the Tujue. Poorly planned and fiercely resisted by the Korean people, Yang Di's northern expeditions proved disastrous. Meanwhile, back in China, growing popular discontent with the emperor's costly military crusades and oppressive forced-labor system led to widespread rebellions. By 618, rebel forces had murdered the much-loathed Yang Di, and the Sui dynasty ended, barely three decades after its founding. The Sui's successor, the brilliant and powerful Tang dynasty, would rule China for three centuries.

The Tang dynasty's leadership thought the wall was a symbol of weakness that merely provided a false sense of security. They allowed the Wall to fall into disrepair and instead focused on diplomacy and trade along the Silk Road, seen here next to the ruins of the Great Wall.

THE TANG REJECT WALL BUILDING

In common with the Sui ruling house, the Tang dynasty was established by a rebel general of mixed Chinese and Xian Bei ancestry. As Patricia Buckley Ebrey has pointed out, however, because both the Sui and the Tang founders had Chinese surnames, they were able to "present themselves as scions [descendants] of old Chinese stock" and as the legitimate heirs to the last great native dynasty to rule China, the Han.[51] During the Sui and Tang eras, "northern China's Xian Bei presence rapidly faded as the Xian Bei were assimilated [absorbed into Chinese culture and society] and their language disappeared."[52]

Not long after assuming power in 618, the Tang founder relinquished the throne in favor of his dynamic son Taizong. One of the most admired rulers in Chinese history, Taizong skillfully combined diplomacy with military force to undermine the Tujue empire. Determined to set Tang boundaries at the greatest

level allowed by military, administrative, and economic con-
straints, Taizong not only recovered the entire Ordos region for
China but also seized much of present-day Inner Mongolia and
southern Manchuria. Turning his attention westward, Taizong
reclaimed the long-lost military and political influence that the
Han dynasty had once wielded in Xinjiang although during Tang
times, few ordinary Chinese settled either in that desolate region
or in the newly acquired steppe territories to the north of the
Chinese heartland. In Central Asia, Tang garrisons were established as far away as Kashgar and other oasis towns on the western side of the vast Takla Makan Desert to protect merchants
from bandits, and trade along the Silk Road flourished as never
before.

As the Middle Kingdom grew stronger militarily and
expanded its borders deep into traditional nomadic territory, the
Great Wall became utterly meaningless as a political boundary.
Scorning the fortifications as a waste of money and effort and a
symbol of military weakness, Taizong lost all interest in repairing or patrolling the walls erected by his predecessors. When one
of his top generals defeated the Tujue in a crucial battle, the
emperor reportedly told him, "You are a better Great Wall than
the one built by Yang Di."[53] In stark contrast to their Sui,
Northern Qi, Northern Wei, Han, and Qin predecessors, the
Tang rulers believed that rigorous military offensives were the
only effective strategy against aggressive neighbors; defensive
walls merely provided a false sense of security.

The Tang leadership's negative view of the Great Wall was mir-
rored in the popular literature of the day. Poetry, along with art,
music, and scholarship flourished under the long-lasting and culturally open dynasty, and even today, the works of the leading
Tang poets are studied and admired in China and throughout
the world. For the Tang writers, the massive northern barricade
was not a symbol of China's grandeur but rather of death and
despair—of the hundreds of thousands of fallen workers
allegedly entombed within its bowels and the aching loneliness
of the soldiers compelled to guard its remotest reaches. In

"Under a Border-Fortress," the celebrated Tang poet Wang Changling used the Great Wall's crumbling ruins as an emblem of the fleeting nature of man's existence and the ultimate futility of his earthly endeavors:

> Drink, my horse, while we cross the autumn water!
> The stream is cold and the wind like a sword,
> As we watch the sunset on the sandy plain,
> Far, far away, shadowy Lintao.
> Old battles, waged by those long walls,
> Once were proud on all men's tongues.
> But antiquity now is a yellow dust,
> Confusing in the grasses its ruins and white bones.[54]

WALL BUILDING IS REVIVED BY A NEW INNER ASIAN DYNASTY

For two centuries, the Tang empire remained free from nomadic invasions. By the late ninth century, however, the central government had been gravely weakened by a series of rebellions, and the territories acquired by Emperor Taizong in Central Asia, Inner Mongolia, and Manchuria were rapidly falling to new Turkish-speaking tribes in the far west and to other nomadic groups in the north, especially the Khitan federation. By the time of the dynasty's collapse in 907, virtually the entire line of the Great Wall, which had once lain well within the boundaries of the vast Tang empire, was again under non-Chinese control.

Following five decades of chaos and nearly constant fighting, most of the Chinese heartland was finally reunited by the Song dynasty (960–1279), one of the most advanced of the Chinese ruling houses culturally but one of the feeblest militarily. Under Song rule, the Khitan federation (now calling itself the Liao dynasty) was able to extend its influence well southward of the arbitrary border of earth and stone first established by Qin Shi Huang Di and into Shanxi and Hebei provinces. After several disastrous attempts to push the intruders back north of the Great Wall, the Song emperor signed a humiliating treaty with the Liao emperor, agreeing to pay him a large annual subsidy of silk and silver in return for peaceful relations. Meanwhile, in the northwest, another non-Chinese alliance led by the Tangut, a people related to the Tibetans, had set up their own state in the Ordos region and modern Gansu province, and the Song eventually found themselves buying peace with tribute from these nomadic rivals as well.

By the beginning of the twelfth century, a third powerful Inner Asian federation, led by the seminomadic Jurchen tribe of eastern Manchuria, had moved south of the Great Wall into the Chinese heartland and was putting added pressure on the already beleaguered Song dynasty. In a remarkably short span of time, the warlike Jurchen had conquered the Khitan empire in Manchuria and northeastern China and established their own Chinese-style dynasty, the Jin. Finally, in 1127, they pushed the Song completely out of northern China.

After forcing the Song court to retreat south of the Yangzi River, the Jurchen drew a new arbitrary border deep within the traditional Chinese heartland. All territory north of the Yangzi was to be the realm of the Jurchen; all to the south would be the Song empire. Adding insult to injury, northern China's newest tribal conquerors pressured the Song emperor to sign a treaty in which he agreed to pay them an annual tribute of 200,000 bolts of silk and large quantities of silver and recognize the Jin as a superior state. Nonetheless, like their Inner Asian predecessors the Northern Wei and Qi, most of the thousands of Jurchen who were resettled south of the Great Wall by their government during the 1100's to aid in controlling the native Chinese quickly took up Chinese ways. Although the traditional Jurchen tribal structure and other Jurchen customs were retained north of the wall in Manchuria, by the time their dynasty collapsed in 1234, most Jurchens residing in the Chinese heartland "spoke Chinese, wore Chinese clothes, used Chinese-style surnames, and married with the local population. A century later, hardly anyone claiming to be Jurchen could be found in China proper, though there still were some in the original homelands in Manchuria."[55]

In addition to adopting Chinese clothing styles, rituals,

farming practices, and writing, the Jin also revived the old Chinese practice of defensive wall building, becoming the first ruling group in the Middle Kingdom to adopt wall building in a big way since the demise of the Sui dynasty nearly 500 years earlier. Because the Jurchens' empire encompassed Manchuria and Inner Mongolia along with the northern half of China, the Great Wall cut straight through the middle of their huge domain. Even though the wall had lost its original purpose as a political and military boundary, the Jin leadership cautiously renovated large sections of the barricade as an inner line of defense against invaders, paying particular attention to the segment of the wall just outside their capital city of Yanjing (modern-day Beijing). The Jurchen also constructed some 500 miles of new walls much farther north than the border ramparts of their Chinese predecessors where no geographical barriers such as high mountains or broad rivers shielded the lands they had seized from other tribal groups during the decades before they conquered northern China. Entirely constructed from earth, the Jurchen's artificial northern barriers traversed portions of Manchuria, Inner Mongolia, and the Mongolian Republic. Today, few traces of the earthen fortifications that once marked the Jin Empire's arbitrary borders with their rivals in the steppe remain because "the region is swept by sand-laden storms and heavy snows."[56]

THE MONGOL CONQUEST

From the beginning of the thirteenth century, the northern threat that most concerned the Jin leadership came from the mighty new steppe federation led by the Mongol warrior Genghis (Chinggis) Khan. After his father, a tribal chieftain, died around 1180, the charismatic young Genghis won the loyalty of his parent's followers and began to assemble an army, which he used to attack and plunder rival tribes in the Mongolian steppe with enormous success. A talented and totally ruthless military commander, Genghis once declared that life's greatest pleasures were slaughtering one's enemies, stealing their cattle and horses, and raping their wives and daughters. In 1206, in recognition of

In the 13th century, the Mongol warrior Genghis Khan conquered large sections of China and Central Asia. Genghis was a ruthless and violent warrior, as seen in this depiction of Genghis and his army capturing a Chinese town.

his outstanding military and leadership skills, Genghis was proclaimed the universal ruler, or great khan, of all steppe peoples. Disregarding old clan and tribal loyalties, the great khan reorganized his highly trained and disciplined cavalry into groups of tens, hundreds, and thousands. Soon afterward, he launched one of the most extraordinary campaigns of conquest in human history.

By 1211, having conquered the nomadic Tangut state in northwestern China, Genghis turned his attention to a far greater prize: the vast empire of the Jurchen. Paralyzed by an internal rebellion, the Jin leadership could mount little resistance. The Mongol forces easily pushed through the defensive walls built by the Jin and their Chinese predecessors until they approached the Jurchen capital of Yanjing. At the heavily fortified gate of Juyongguan, just north of Yangjing, Genghis Khan's cavalry was brought to a standstill. Following a lengthy siege, the Mongols finally burst through only to discover that the capital city was protected by even more formidable fortifications, including 40-foot-high walls and an impressive complex of moats, watchtowers, and huge stone forts. After the Jurchen turned back two separate attempts to storm the defenses, Genghis withdrew his forces. Four years later the Mongols were back. With the assistance of collaborators within the capital, they were at last able to capture Yanjing though not before the Jin court had managed to flee southward to modern Henan province. Thousands of Yanjing's inhabitants were massacred as a warning to the Jurchen's other walled cities, and according to one account, the ravaged capital burned for more than a month.

After sacking Yangjing, Genghis Khan led his army westward again, seizing several wealthy Central Asian cities. Following Genghis's death at the age of 60 in 1227, his battle-hardened forces pushed even further westward, conquering Russia and invading Poland, Bohemia, and Hungary. In the meantime, the new great khan, Genghis's son Ogodei, resumed his father's earlier conquests in East Asia, invading Korea and finally crushing the Jin dynasty once and for all in 1234. Now only the Song dynasty in southern China was left to challenge Mongol control of the Middle Kingdom. By 1236, Ogodei had taken a grave toll on the Song empire, conquering most of present-day Sichuan province and slaughtering more than one million men, women, and children in the major southern metropolis of Chengdu after city leaders refused to surrender to his forces.

Ogodei, nevertheless, hesitated to launch an all-out attack on southern China, probably because the region's many rivers, streams, and canals posed a formidable barrier to mounted forces. Not until Genghis's enterprising grandson Khubilai was appointed as the great khan in 1260 would the Mongol conquest of the Song begin in earnest. For more than a decade, Khubilai's forces campaigned against the Song, finally defeating them in 1279. With the end of the Song dynasty, the entire Middle Kingdom was under the control of a non-Chinese people for the first time in its long history.

MONGOL RULE

"The traditional view of Mongol rule over China was that it was an unmitigated [total] disaster," notes J.A.G. Roberts.[57] In truth, Mongol rule was not all bad. Khubilai Khan generously supported Chinese science and the performing arts, improved the country's postal relay system, significantly extended the Grand Canal, constructed many miles of new roads, and promoted trade between the newly reunited north and south. He also reinvigorated the Middle Kingdom's foreign commerce by assigning soldiers to guard merchants traveling on the Silk Road and encouraging southeastern China's fledgling maritime (seagoing) trade.

The growth in international trade under Mongol rule led to the first direct contacts between Europe and the Middle Kingdom. Many Western missionaries and traders, including the famed Venetian merchant Marco Polo, visited Khubilai's court. Through the reports of these intrepid globetrotters, and particularly through the best-selling *Travels of Marco Polo*, Europe learned of the grandeur of China's cities and of amazing Chinese inventions such as printing and gunpowder. One of China's many wonders that Polo failed to mention in his book, however, was the Great Wall. Perhaps Polo's puzzling omission was based on a desire "not to clutter his volume with details of things which had no real function in [Mongol] China."[58] The Mongol conquest had brought China into a global empire that extended from Eastern Europe through Russia and Western Asia all the way to the Sea of Japan. Consequently, as far as the Middle Kingdom's newest rulers were concerned, the defensive walls that Qin Shi Huang Di and his successors had built to mark and protect China's various borders with Inner Asia over the centuries had "lost any usefulness."[59]

Although Khubilai Khan took a Chinese name for his new dynasty, the Yuan, and moved the capital of the Mongol's empire from the steppe to Beijing, unlike earlier invaders such as the Xian Bei and the Jurchen, the Mongols determinedly resisted assimilation into Chinese culture and society. Officials carried out their business in the Mongol language; traditional steppe clothing styles, foods, and religious practices were retained; and intermarriage between Mongols and Chinese was strictly forbidden.

Just as the Mongols did not take up Chinese ways, under the Yuan, "the Chinese were not forced to adopt the customs of their conquerors."[60] Nonetheless, the Mongols made a point of treating their Chinese subjects as inferiors. Chinese were relegated to minor positions in the government with the important posts being held by Mongols and Central or Western Asians, including many Turks. Hundreds of thousands of Chinese had their farm fields seized by Mongol authorities and were forced into slavery or serfdom. Moreover, Chinese paid higher taxes than Mongols, could not possess weapons or walk the streets after dark, and were punished more severely than Mongols for similar crimes.

After the death of the capable and forceful Khubilai Khan in 1294, a series of succession disputes weakened the Mongol government in Beijing and its authority declined steadily. Eager to take advantage of this weakness at the center, the Chinese people rose up against their Mongol oppressors, organizing ever larger and more powerful resistance movements. Finally, in 1368, a youthful peasant leader from southern China overthrew the last of the Yuan emperors. When the much-despised Yuan dynasty collapsed, "the Mongols in China did not simply melt into the

Chinese population the way the Xian Bei and Jurchen had. Rather, those who could escape fled northward back to the steppe."[61]

With the hated Mongols finally gone and the establishment of the new Ming dynasty by a young southern peasant leader (Emperor Hong Wu), all of the Chinese heartland was under Chinese control for the first time in more than 400 years. Once again, China's rulers were confronted with the perennial ques-

THE MONGOLS AND THE CHINESE

The Chinese have long considered the nearly 90-year-long Yuan dynasty as one of the darkest periods in their history. In Chinese eyes, one of the most detestable acts of the Yuan's founder, Khubilai Khan, was his separation of the Middle Kingdom's population into four categories. Under Kubilai Khan's system, the Mongols were at the apex of the social and political pyramid, followed by their allies from Central and Western Asia including Persians, Turks, and Tibetans. The third level comprised former subjects of the Jurchen empire in northern China, and at the very bottom, were the recently conquered southern Chinese. This ethnic classification system profoundly affected a person's ability to attain public office, the amount of taxes he had to pay, and how he was treated before the law. Chinese subjects, for example, could expect to be severely punished if they dared to fight back when assaulted by a Mongol whereas a Mongol who murdered a Chinese merely had to pay a fine. According to Marco Polo, Mongol authorities once ordered the massacre of the entire population of a city near the Yangzi River in retribution for the killing of several unruly, drunken Mongol soldiers by a small group of Chinese.

The Chinese were deeply angered and insulted by these inequities under Mongol rule, especially because most considered the Mongols to be their cultural inferiors. To the Chinese, the Mongol leadership appeared ignorant and uncouth. Many were illiterate; they scorned bathing and liked to sleep outside in tents on the palace grounds. At their raucous state banquets, they gorged themselves on cheese, horse's milk, and other steppe foods that the Chinese considered disgusting, used "barbaric" steel knives to cut their meat, and made spectacles of themselves by indulging in too much *kumiss* (an alcoholic drink made from mare's milk).

tion of where their own empire should end and the realm of the Inner Asian nomad begin. As it turned out, the long-neglected Great Wall and the arbitrary border between Chinese and nomad that it represented would play a critical role in the Ming response to that age-old question.

6

The
Ming Wall

The new Ming dynasty's peasant founder, Hong Wu (reigned 1368–1398) was determined to revive the grandeur of China's imperial tradition and erase all vestiges of Mongol rule. Heeding the saying "learn from the Tang and Song," he enthusiastically reintroduced Chinese customs and rites at court, even going so far as to decree that the clothing and hairstyles worn by his subjects strictly follow Tang dynasty models.[62]

A "firm believer in the absolute power of the monarchy," Hong Wu was a tyrannical ruler.[63] Under his reign, the imperial government became more autocratic and centralized than ever before. Fearful of rivals and deeply suspicious of just about everyone, Hong Wu abolished the key post of prime minister and ordered massive purges of government officials and army leaders. Tens of thousands of Chinese lost their lives in the emperor's brutal purges; many others were sentenced to years of forced labor.

Split into a number of different confederations and lacking strong leaders, the Mongols did not pose a serious threat to China during Hong Wu's reign. Nevertheless, paranoid that the Mongols would reunite and overrun China again, Hong Wu maintained a vigilant watch on his kingdom's northern frontiers. The first Ming emperor established a string of military outposts on the fringes of the steppe, just to the north of the Great Wall. He also sent several military expeditions deep into the grasslands in hopes of driving the various Mongol tribes as far from northern China as possible.

THE USURPER YONG LE

In 1398, following the death of the Ming founder, Hong Wu's teenage grandson and designated successor was proclaimed emperor. By 1403, however, the young monarch had mysteriously disappeared, and his uncle—Hong Wu's ruthless fourth son Yong Le—had become China's ruler. Keenly sensitive to charges that he had usurped (illegally seized) the throne from his father's rightful heir, the new emperor promptly "launched a series of ambitious policies designed to demonstrate his own greatness."[64]

The most famous of Yong Le's grandiose schemes were the oceanic expeditions he sponsored to Vietnam, Indonesia, India, and the eastern coast of Africa, a century before the more famous voyages of the European explorers Christopher Columbus and Vasco da Gama. The purpose of Yong Le's far-flung maritime expeditions was neither to obtain territory nor to carry on private trade, which was banned throughout much of the Ming era. Instead, the accused usurper seems to have launched the costly voyages out of a desire to boost his own standing and authority by having as many foreign rulers as possible formally recognize him as China's emperor. After Yong Le's death in 1424, his successors soon abandoned his expensive naval ventures, a decision that would have "disastrous long-term consequences" for the Middle Kingdom in the centuries ahead, notes one historian, by "leaving China's long coastline unprotected against ... the more aggressive European traders from the West."[65]

Yong Le's ambitious foreign policy was directed at the steppe as well as the sea. Intent on enhancing his own status and power by expanding the empire's boundaries northward, Yong Le personally led five military expeditions into the heart of the Mongolian steppe to fight the Oirat and Tatar (often misspelled as "Tartar") tribes, the two largest nomad groups of the time. Chasing down the fast-riding horsemen in Inner Asia's vast expanses and provisioning his troops with food and other supplies during the distant campaigns proved extremely difficult and costly for Yong Le. Consequently, following the emperor's death, Yong Le's successors abandoned his crusade to conquer Mongolia for the Middle Kingdom along with his expensive naval ventures.

THE DEBACLE AT TUMU

Under the Mongol Yuan dynasty, trade had flourished between Inner Asia and China, meaning that the nomadic peoples of the steppe could readily obtain the agricultural and manufactured goods they desired but could not produce for themselves. Far

The Ming dynasty was founded in the fourteenth century, and its leaders were determined to protect China from another attack by Mongol forces. In this painting, the cavalry of the Ming Emperor Zhengtong charges into battle against the Mongols.

less interested in trading with their northern neighbors than their Mongol predecessors had been, the Ming rulers substantially decreased commercial exchanges between their kingdom and the steppe. Indeed, many within the Ming regime scorned Inner Asians as their cultural and moral inferiors and wanted the

Chinese Empire to have as little to do with them as possible, either economically or diplomatically.

Although the nomads remained disunited and relatively weak throughout the reigns of Hong Wu and Yong Le, during the two decades following Yong Le's death, a bold Oirat chieftain named Esen formed a new federation of Mongol tribes. In 1449, Esen, infuriated by the Ming government's refusal to meet his demands for increased trade and diplomatic ties, sent a huge raiding party into northern Shanxi province. Thousands of Chinese civilians and soldiers were killed or captured. The 22-year-old Ming emperor Zhengtong, against the objections of most of his advisers, resolved to lead a "punitive expedition" to put the Mongol "bandits" in their place.[66]

The young emperor's expedition was an unqualified disaster. Despite his supreme confidence in the ability of his forces to put the Mongol "bandits" in their place, the Chinese army of Zhengtong's time was not what it had been under his Ming predecessors, Hong Wu and Yong Le. Discipline had declined, and "riding and archery"—skills that were essential in fighting the nomads—"were being forgotten".[67] Seventy miles northwest of the Ming capital at Beijing, at the remote postal relay station of Tumu, Zhengtong's large but poorly organized and trained forces marched directly into an Oirat ambush. In one of the most infamous routs in Chinese history, the panic-stricken imperial army, which reportedly numbered a half million, was slaughtered almost to a man. According to an eyewitness account, as his men were being "cut to pieces" by the enemy, the emperor "dismounts and sits on the ground amidst a hail of arrows that kills most of his attendants. He remains unharmed and waits calmly."[68] Esen's forces then captured China's supreme ruler and triumphantly carried him back to Mongolia with them.

To the Oirats' surprise, Zhengtong's top officials decided to ignore Esen's ransom demands and abandon their kidnapped ruler, enthroning his younger brother in his place. The next year a disappointed Esen released Zhengtong, who was eventually able to reclaim the Ming throne following a bitter succession dispute. The Mongols had failed to exact any significant trade or diplomatic concessions from the Chinese as a consequence of their victory in 1449, but the Tumu debacle would nonetheless have a dramatic and lasting impact on Ming strategy toward the steppe.

SETTING THE STAGE FOR THE MING GREAT WALL: THE DEBATE OVER NATIONAL SECURITY POLICY

In the wake of the Chinese army's devastating rout at Tumu, the Ming regime was compelled to reevaluate its foreign policy. Although virtually everyone in the administration agreed that the Mongols were China's chief national security concern, there was considerable disagreement among the leadership regarding how to best deal with China's dangerous neighbors to the north. The Ming officials debated three possible solutions to the nomad problem, none of which were completely satisfactory, as the leading authority on Ming policy toward the Mongols points out.

One option was a preemptive strike. The imperial army would invade the steppe and crush the Mongol forces before they had a chance to organize another attack on Chinese territory. The pro-war bloc argued that the Chinese "should take advantage of their military strengths," including their unmatched "knowledge of firearms," to vanquish the nomads on their own turf. They could then maintain an occupying force in southern Inner Asia to safeguard the Chinese heartland's "strategic periphery."[69] (The Chinese had invented gunpowder as far back as the tenth century but had only begun using firearms extensively in battle during the Ming era). To follow any other course of action, argued one pro-war official, "may be compared to attempting to stop water from boiling without knowing enough to remove the firewood; it will not stop catastrophes along the border."[70] Still, many Ming officials—military as well as civilian—hesitated to adopt an aggressive stance toward the steppe. As Emperor Yong Le's futile attempts to conquer the

Mongols decades earlier and the recent fiasco at Tumu had demonstrated all too clearly, offensive campaigning in the vast expanses of Inner Asia was extremely arduous, costly, and dangerous.

The second option that the Ming considered for controlling the nomads centered on trade and diplomacy. Meeting the Mongols' long-standing demands for closer trading and diplomatic relations between the Middle Kingdom and Inner Asia, some statesmen maintained, was the most cost-effective and least risky way to bring peace to northern China. Deeply distrustful of their nomadic neighbors, however, many court officials strenuously objected to establishing stronger economic and political ties with the steppe. Giving the Mongols the goods they desired would merely serve to strengthen them, they argued, and Mongol trade or diplomatic missions to China would provide a convenient cover for nomad spies to infiltrate the Middle Kingdom. Convinced that the nomads were their cultural and moral inferiors, other Chinese officials scorned the strategy of trying to manage the northern "barbarians" peacefully through diplomacy and trade as an affront to the dignity of the Ming emperor and his subjects. These policymakers were fond of quoting the celebrated Han statesman Jia Yi who had denounced the old he qin strategy of buying peace from the nomads with royal marriages and costly gifts. Jia Yi argued that this strategy was contrary to the Heaven-appointed order in which the Chinese sovereign "should remain on the top" and the "barbarians" and their "insolent" leaders "should be placed at the bottom."[71]

The final foreign policy alternative debated in the Ming court following the defeat at Tumu focused on defense and exclusion—in other words, wall building. If military conquest was impracticable and diplomacy and trade were unsuitable—even demeaning—then rebuilding and remanning the northern fortifications of the Qin, Sui, and other past dynasties, appeared to many officials as the sole course left for them to follow. Echoing the arguments put forth by the Northern Wei statesman Gao Lu some 1,000 years earlier in his memorial, "In Favor of Long Walls," the pro-wall faction contended that whereas the nomads excelled at riding and lightning-fast attacks, the Chinese excelled at defense. Like the other two strategies considered by the Ming court, defensive wall building also had its opponents. Wall building was a tremendous waste of money and human resources, these critics argued, pointing out that China's northern ramparts had failed to keep the Mongols out, not to mention earlier northern conquerors such as the Jurchens. According to Jonathan Fryer, the supporters of wall building countered by asserting that if the Great Wall had never been built, "China would be on the receiving end of nomad attacks every season instead of experiencing only a few major invasions every century."[72]

As the faction-ridden Ming regime continued to squabble over the best solution—offensive, diplomatic, or defensive—to the "barbarian" threat, the Mongols steadily became stronger, exerting more and more pressure on China's northern borders, particularly in the long-disputed Ordos region of the Yellow River loop. Finally, in 1472, nearly 25 years after the Tumu rout, Oriat horsemen swept through the eroding and poorly manned section of the wall to the west of the Ordos and claimed most of the territory within the Yellow River's great bend. Too weak to force the Oriats out of the Ordos and too proud to negotiate with a people they viewed as their moral and cultural inferiors, the Ming regime finally committed itself to defensive wall construction as a compromise. According to Arthur Waldron, this "turn toward extensive wall-building" following decades of bickering and indecision "probably reflected the fact that all contenders could agree on it, despite its doubtful military merits."[73]

THE GREATEST CHINESE BORDER WALL

In 1474, the Ming dynasty began work on a new frontier barrier on the fringes of the Ordos region. The new barricade's chief purpose was to block potential Mongol invasion routes from the Ordos into China proper and particularly to the capital city of

Beijing. It also created a new arbitrary border for north-central China, one that lay miles south of the old Sui defense line that cut diagonally across the Ordos and was many more miles below Qin Shi Huang Di's border ramparts on the northern side of the Yellow River's bend. The Ming leadership evidently believed that China no longer possessed the military or economic where-withal to control the grasslands and fertile plains of the Ordos' northern sector, valuable territory that many of their more pow-erful and confident predecessors—from Qin Shi Huang Di to Taizong—had once claimed for the Middle Kingdom.

Over the next half century, Ming wall construction moved steadily eastward, focusing primarily on the areas surrounding the dynasty's capital at Beijing. Like China's earlier defensive walls, these early Ming ramparts were erected by huge work gangs of soldiers and civilian draftees using the age-old hang-tu or rammed earth technique. In contrast to the first Ming wall in the Ordos region, much of the construction now followed the line of the crumbling border ramparts of previous ruling houses, including the Great Wall's original builders, the Qin. By the middle of the 1500s, the Ming regime was investing more heavily in its great northern barrier than ever before. For the first time, significant portions of the Great Wall were being con-structed from stone—generally granite—and many of its earthen sections were being faced with stone or brick. Numerous inner and secondary walls were also constructed; in some areas three parallel sections of ramparts were raised.

The dynasty's commitment to building a stronger and more imposing Great Wall from the mid-sixteenth century onward was undoubtedly linked to the rise of a new menace in the north—the ambitious and fiercely proud Mongol leader, Altan Khan. To secure supplies and soldiers for their ongoing cam-paign against their rivals, the Oirats, Altan Khan and his horse-men repeatedly raided Chinese frontier communities. During a series of border raids in 1542, they allegedly killed or captured 200,000 Chinese and seized a million head of horses and cattle. Three decades later, under the direction of an unusually flexible

The Ming dynasty committed to rebuilding and reinforcing the Great Wall in hopes of defending northern China and Beijing from aggressive Mongol and nomad tribes. Construction of the new wall lasted almost three hundred years, and the completed Ming wall stretched 1,700 miles and was thirty-five feet tall and twenty feet wide in places.

Ming official named Zhang Juzheng, the Chinese government finally made peace with Altan Khan by promising trade and diplomatic concessions, including conferring the rank of prince on the imperious Mongol leader. Zhang Juzheng's willingness to negotiate with the Mongols was clearly not based on a belief in their fundamental equality with the Chinese. In a memorial to the Ming emperor, Zhang Juzheng recommended that he treat the nomads as a master would his vicious dog:

> The important principle is for the officials in charge to deal with them in a flexible manner: Just like dogs, if they wag their tails, bones will be thrown to them; if they bark wildly, they will be beaten with sticks; after the beating, if they sub-

mit again, bones will be thrown to them again, then more beating.[74]

Even after establishing peaceful relations with Altan Khan, the Ming government, fearful that another northern threat was sure to arise sooner or later, continued to invest heavily in fortifying its northern borders, particularly in the sector of the Great Wall between Beijing and the Yellow Sea. The most impressive stretch of the Ming wall ran along the low yet rugged mountains just to the north of the capital city. There the wall measured up to 35 feet in height and up to 20 feet in width along its paved top, providing room for Chinese defenders to move troops, horses, and equipment quickly and easily from one part of the fortifications to another in case of attack. Numerous watchtowers, forts, and beacon (signal) towers were built not only along the strategically vital sections of the wall near Beijing but along the entire structure. By the early 1600s, the wall stretched for some 1,700 miles from Shanhaiguan on the coast of the Yellow Sea to the remote fortress of Jiayuguan in northwestern Gansu province. The Ming wall's western terminus—and China's newest arbitrary borderline in the northwest—lay more than 400 miles east of the Han wall's eroded terminus in Xinjiang. Clearly, the ever-cautious Ming rulers' vision of where the Chinese Empire should end was far narrower than that of the ambitious and dynamic Emperor Wu Di.

The string of lofty brick and stone beacon towers that the Ming constructed at regular intervals (often as close as a half mile apart) on and just to the south of their Great Wall were an especially vital part of their border fortifications. "To have any sort of advantage over the nomads," noted one scholar, "the Ming needed to know of a threat as soon as possible; systems of fire, smoke, and sound signals, relayed from tower to tower across hundreds of miles of desert and mountain, ensured that they did."[75] The Ming, like the Han and Qin dynasties, committed large numbers of soldiers to guarding their Great Wall. Nonetheless, given the enormous length of China's northern frontier, small units of no more than 20 soldiers manned the wall's many watchtowers; even the barrier's passes (major strongholds) were typically guarded by units of only a few thousand troops. Hence, rapid communication of enemy

THE GREAT WALL AS A COMMUNICATION SYSTEM

One of the Great Wall's most critical functions was to pass warnings of invasion and other messages by means of its many beacon or signal towers. Capable of relaying information far more rapidly than a rider on horseback, the wall's beacon system could convey messages over a distance of several hundred miles within a matter of hours.

When the Ming government first acquired the large guns from Portuguese traders during the seventeenth century, signaling was sometimes carried out by firing cannon, but smoke and fire signals remained the usual method of passing messages along the Great Wall throughout the Ming era. The beacon communication system was first developed during the Qin and Han dynasties when fixed numbers of beacon fires were employed as a code to report the size of invading armies to garrisons stationed along the Great Wall. Under the Ming, one beacon fire indicated an invading force of up to 100 horsemen, two signaled a force of up to 500, three meant more than 1,000 invaders had been sighted, and four beacon fires indicated an enemy army of 5,000 or more.

Because accurate communication was of crucial importance to the defense of China's long northern border, the beacon towers and the units of up to 20 soldiers who manned them were closely supervised. Delay in sending information or absence from beacon tower duty without permission were strictly prohibited. A decree issued by the Ming Emperor Cheng Hua stipulated that:

The beacon towers, together with their guards, must be inspected regularly. Stocks must be stored in quantity, and lookouts placed around the clock. In case of emergency, raise smoke in the daytime, or light a fire by night, to pass on the alert. See to it that no damage is done to the towers, so as to ensure prompt communication. Those who convey the information quickly and help defeat the enemy will be rewarded. Violators shall be punished according to military law.*

*Quoted in Luo Zewen, Dai Wenbao, Dick Wilson, J. P. Drege, and H. Delahaye, *The Great Wall*, (New York: McGraw-Hill, 1981), p. 152.

attack followed by equally rapid mobilization and deployment of additional troops to counterattack was essential to the Ming defense system.

THE HIGH COSTS OF MING WALL BUILDING

Constructing the strongest and most elaborate border fortifications in the history of Chinese defensive wall building required massive investments of money and manpower. Utilizing bricks and stone blocks to construct the wall and its thousands of forts, beacon towers, watchtowers, and other structures substantially increased the cost of the Middle Kingdom's border defenses since the employment of brickmakers, stone masons, and other specialized craftsmen was now required. Adding to the government's expenses, a "considerable network of brick-kilns, quarries, and transportation routes" also would have had to be developed.[76]

In addition to the teams of skilled craftsmen who worked on the Ming Great Wall, millions of soldiers and convicted criminals also toiled on the sprawling defense line. "Worker numbers mushroomed during the Ming dynasty, in order to cope with the vastly increased scale and extent of construction," writes a modern expert on the Great Wall:

> Armies were enlarged and a new penal code established to ensure a constant supply of manpower for the work. Scores of offenses were met with sentences of labor on the Great Wall. Even petty criminals were given life terms of work on the structure. More serious offenders received 'perpetual' sentences. This meant that after the convict died working on the Great Wall, a member of his family—a son, brother, cousin or nephew—was sought as a replacement, inheriting the sentence. During the Ming dynasty, censuses gave officials accurate information on the populace and family relationships, thus providing the administrative basis for operating such a draconian penal system.[77]

Under the Ming, no less than 200 different offenses carried

the sentence of hard labor on the Great Wall either "perpetually" or for life.

As was true during earlier periods of massive wall construction under prior dynasties, hundreds of thousands of the Ming wall's laborers succumbed to exhaustion, disease, malnutrition, or accidents. According to popular tradition, the white color of the mortar that bound the Ming wall's bricks together acquired its shade from the pulverized bones of fallen workers. In some Chinese villages near the wall, the mortar was popularly believed to possess miraculous powers for healing all sorts of ailments. (Recently, researchers discovered that the Ming wall's mortar actually derived both its white color and its remarkable strength from a secret ingredient: rice flour.)

THE DECLINE OF THE MING AND THE MANCHU CONQUEST

During the sixteenth and early seventeenth centuries, Ming China was ruled by a series of weak and incompetent emperors. Perhaps the most inept of these was Wanli, who reigned for nearly a half century from 1573 until his death in 1620. Irresponsible and self-absorbed, Wanli withdrew more and more from state affairs over the course of his long reign. Important governmental posts throughout the empire were left vacant and in many areas, the entire administrative system was paralyzed. Although he invested heavily in extending and renovating the Great Wall, particularly near Beijing, Wanli allocated virtually no money for repairing flood dikes and other essential projects. To pay for his lavish wardrobe and palaces, the pleasure-loving emperor instituted burdensome new taxes. Nonetheless, by the final years of his reign, the empire was virtually bankrupt. As China's financial situation deteriorated, even Wanli's pet project, the Great Wall, was neglected. Renovation efforts ground to a halt and many of the wall's defenders, left without provisions or pay, deserted their posts along the northern fortifications.

By the time of Wanli's death in 1620, the empire was on the brink of collapse as popular revolts against the Ming dynasty's inefficient and corrupt rule spread across the countryside.

Meanwhile, a new threat to the Middle Kingdom was developing in the plains and forests of Manchuria to the northeast of the Chinese heartland. There, the Manchu, a fishing, hunting, and farming people descended from northern China's twelfth-century conquerors, the Jurchen, had built a powerful tribal federation and begun to set their sights on the rich kingdom to their south.

On April 24, 1644, after Chinese rebel forces attacked the seat of Ming power in Beijing, the Manchu saw their chance to extend their burgeoning empire into the wealthy Chinese heartland. With the imperial army in disarray and popular support for their regime virtually nonexistent, the Ming were powerless to resist the rebels and that same night the dynasty's last emperor committed suicide. Determined to take advantage of the chaos in China's capital, Manchu troops began advancing toward Beijing. After a renegade Chinese general let their huge army pass through the gates of the easternmost section of the Great Wall at Shanhaiguan, the Manchu swept down on Beijing's new rebel regime and claimed the capital—and the Chinese Empire—for themselves.

The Manchu conquest meant more than the end of the Ming dynasty; it also meant the end of any meaningful role for the Great Wall as either a national boundary or a defensive system. The domain of the Qing, as the Manchu called their new Chinese-style dynasty, extended well north and west of the Great Wall. It encompassed Manchuria (which by 1800 had been heavily settled by Chinese immigrants from the south and officially incorporated into the empire as the "northeastern provinces"), Inner Mongolia, Xinjiang Uighur Autonomous Region, and Tibet, as well as much of today's Mongolian Republic. Ironically, under the rule of the Manchu, a people whom most Chinese continued to consider as foreigners even long after they had adopted Chinese political, religious, and social customs, the Chinese Empire's territorial boundaries would reach their greatest extent. The Qing dynasty was able to control so much northern and western territory because Manchu forces had conquered their tribe's chief rivals in Inner Asia, the Mongols, during the decade before the Manchu invaded the Middle Kingdom. By closely supervising the steppe politically and forcing the various Mongol tribes to remain in certain fixed areas, the Qing dynasty ensured that the Mongols would never again pose a threat to the Middle Kingdom. Consequently, under Qing rule, the Great Wall was left unmanned and soon fell into disrepair.

Nonetheless, the story of the arbitrary earthen and stone boundary first erected by Qin Shi Huang Di to separate the Chinese from their nomadic neighbors was not finished yet. From the sixteenth century on, European traders, diplomats, and missionaries visited China in increasing numbers. They returned home with thrilling accounts of the magnificent Ming Great Wall as well as many misconceptions regarding its construction and true age. The foreigners' sensational reports soon captured the imagination of their compatriots, and by the late nineteenth century a sojourn to the Great Wall had become an essential part of the Western tourist's Chinese itinerary. With the fall of the Qing dynasty—and the entire Chinese imperial system—following the Republican Revolution of 1911–1912, the Great Wall also started to take on a new and enduring significance for the Chinese people themselves. It became a symbol of China's long and rich civilization and even of its national identity.

7

The Great Wall in Western and Chinese Eyes

During the sixteenth and seventeenth centuries, a growing number of merchants from Portugal, the Netherlands, Spain, and other European countries reached the Middle Kingdom by sea routes first discovered by Portuguese explorers in the early 1500s. It was from these intrepid travelers that Europe first learned of the Great Wall. The Westerners' accounts of the huge barrier were admiring in the extreme. According to one contemporary historian, "Visually, the Ming Great Wall, snaking across the crests of ridges and low mountains, crossing defiles [narrow passages between mountains] and valleys where great defensible gateways blocked the roadways, is a familiar image in the modern world's consciousness; it is one that struck awe in the minds of travelers in the past."[78] The "seven wonders of the world put together are not comparable to this work," rhapsodized one seventeenth-century French visitor.[79] Awed by the rampart's colossal proportions, a Russian trader who visited China in 1692 was convinced that the Great Wall was "fifteen fathom [90 feet] high"—more than 50 feet taller than the barrier's highest sections near Beijing.[80]

EAST VERSUS WEST: CHINA'S NEWEST INVADERS

Under the direction of the strong-willed Manchu emperor, Qianlong, the Middle Kingdom began strictly limiting international trade during the early 1700s. Deeply distrustful of foreigners and persuaded that China had no need of the Westerners' "strange and costly objects," Qianlong refused to negotiate treaties of trade and friendship with the European ambassadors who flocked to his court over the course of the emperor's 64-year-reign.[81]

In 1793, eager to acquire lucrative Chinese trade goods such as tea, porcelain, and silk, the English government sent a particularly large diplomatic delegation to Beijing, including more than 90 envoys, craftsmen, and artists. Many of the delegation's members, including its leader, George Macartney, made a point of journeying to the Great Wall, which had been so vividly described by earlier European travelers. Like most other

Westerners, Macartney was under the impression that the entire structure, including the elaborate brick and stone ramparts that he visited just north of Beijing, dated from the long-ago days of the First Sovereign Emperor, Qin Shi Huang Di. Consequently, Macartney was amazed to discover a series of holes—too small to aim crossbows through but just the right size for muskets—along the wall's top. Never imagining that the wall section was of Ming origin and barely 200 years old, Macartney concluded that the Chinese must have already possessed firearms during the Qin dynasty (221–206 B.C.), more than 1,500 years before Europeans first manufactured them.

Although Lord Macartney failed to secure a commercial treaty from Emperor Qianlong, his diplomatic mission attracted a great deal of attention back in Europe. Many members of the large British delegation published popular accounts of their travels in the Middle Kingdom after returning home, complete with thrilling descriptions of the "stupendous" Great Wall.[82] Overwhelmed by the magnitude of the Ming wall section he viewed near Beijing, Macartney's secretary John Barrow calculated that the entire Great Wall contained more bricks and stone than "all the dwelling houses of England and Scotland," and that did not even include the fortification's numerous towers.[83] Barrow's farfetched computation was based on the erroneous but widely held assumption among Westerners that the imposing brick and granite walls they observed in northeastern China extended all the way to the old defense line's western terminus in modern Gansu. In fact, few of the western sections of the Great Wall were faced in stone or brick; most were constructed solely from earth and had eroded significantly by Barrow's day.

In the wake of the well-publicized British mission, Europe's fascination with Chinese culture and appetite for Chinese goods reached unprecedented heights. By the early nineteenth century, exasperated with China's confining trade policies, Western political and commercial leaders resolved to overcome the irksome restrictions by whatever means proved necessary. With the end of Emperor Qianlong's reign in 1799, the time was ripe for

China's newest wave of invaders—Western businessmen and envoys who descended on the Middle Kingdom from the direction of its unprotected ocean border rather than sweeping down from the steppe as the nomadic horsemen had done in earlier times. These interlopers proved even more mobile and determined than the Mongols, and the series of weak and inept emperors who ruled China after the death of the formidable Qianlong could do little to stop them. Intimidated by the Western powers' modernized armies and technological expertise, from the mid-1800s on, the feeble Qing regime allowed the unscrupulous intruders to extort sweeping trade concessions. Westerners gained control of mining rights, railroads, and naval stations in a number of vital areas and even set up their own courts of law in order to elude the Chinese justice system.

TOURING THE GREAT WALL

Ironically, even as their compatriots were humiliating and exploiting the Middle Kingdom, most Westerners remained enthralled by China's rich culture and history, and particularly by its biggest cultural relic: the Great Wall. By the late nineteenth century, Westerners were arriving in China in greater numbers than ever before as the Middle Kingdom became a fashionable destination for the more adventuresome European and American tourists. Most took the time to visit the Great Wall, "a supremely wonderful sight," according to one enthusiastic French visitor.[84] Few Westerners ever saw more of the old defense line than the impressive granite and brick Ming wall just north of the capital city, however. Not until 1909 would one of them, the American author William Edgar Geil, try to traverse the entire course of the Ming Great Wall from Shanhaiguan near the Yellow Sea to the remote fortress of Jiayuguan in modern Gansu province. In his widely read account of the expedition, Geil praised the wall's creators for being "ahead of the senseless militarism of Europe" (which was then locked in an escalating arms race and on the brink of World War I). "A wall to protect the living," he declared, "was better than a ditch to cover the dead."[85]

Although Western tourism in China flourished throughout most of the early 1900s, for a brief time at the very start of the twentieth century, tourist traffic to the Middle Kingdom came to an abrupt halt. In 1900, China erupted in a bloody anti-foreign uprising that would come to be known as the Boxer Rebellion. Led by the Boxers ("righteous fists" in Chinese), a secret society dedicated to ridding the Middle Kingdom of its Western exploiters, the rebellion resulted in the deaths of hundreds of European traders, diplomats, and missionaries. Curiously, the Great Wall played a role, albeit a small one, in the outbreak of the rebellion. Shortly before the uprising began, four Denver journalists concocted a sensational news story about the famous structure. According to the newspapermen, a team of engineers was traveling to China from Denver to demolish the Great Wall, an action supposedly approved by the Qin regime as a symbol of their willingness to open the Middle Kingdom to foreign traders and diplomats. When the phony story found its way to China, the already powerful anti-foreign movement was further strengthened.

Nonetheless, the Boxers' dream of liberating their homeland of the insolent "foreign devils" was soon dashed. In yet another blow to the Middle Kingdom's national pride, a large army of U.S., European, and Japanese troops was sent to China to crush the uprising, an assignment which the foreigners carried out with brutal efficiency. Because it had lent its support to the Boxers, the Qing government was compelled to pay over 300 million dollars in restitution to the foreign nations whose property had been damaged in the rebellion, revise its commercial treaties to make them even more advantageous to the West, and permit the stationing of foreign troops in Beijing.

CHANGING CHINESE PERCEPTIONS OF THE GREAT WALL

An early twentieth-century guidebook intended for European tourists in China confidently asserted that the Great Wall sections near Beijing would "send a thrill of romance through even the most prosaic [unimaginative] Briton, a quickening of the imagination akin to that inspired by the Sphinx and the Pyramids ... or by the decaying glories of Rome and Greece."[86] About the Chinese themselves, however, the guidebook's author noted reproachfully, "the Great Wall seems to have no kindling fire. He regards it with placid indifference, to be venerated, indeed, as ancient, but more especially as handsome proof" that earlier generations must have been considerably better off or they could not have afforded such an extravagant project.[87]

Indeed, as Arthur Waldron noted in his study of the Great Wall, over most of the course of its long history, the Chinese people appear to have taken the massive barricade for granted. The Great Wall was all but ignored by Chinese artists, rarely appearing in the exquisite landscape paintings for which the Middle Kingdom was famous. Few writers took note of the wall either, and most of those who did mention it tended to present the structure in a negative light. The celebrated poets of the Tang dynasty, for example, typically associated the Great Wall with suffering, isolation, and death. The few surviving folk legends about the wall, particularly the famous tale of Meng Jiangnu whose husband died toiling on Qin Shi Huang Di's barrier and was buried within the rampart, also portray the wall in a negative manner. They emphasize the tyranny of its creator and the misery of the peasants who were compelled to build it. For many Chinese writers and scholars, when the greatest defensive wall-building dynasty of all time—the Ming—succumbed to the Manchu invaders from the north, the Great Wall came to symbolize not only despotism and suffering but also military weakness and incompetence.

After the fall of the Manchu Qing dynasty and the establishment of the Chinese Republic in the Revolution of 1911–1912, however, Chinese perceptions of the Great Wall began to change. By the time of the Revolution, Western admiration for the Great Wall had reached unprecedented heights with European and American writers now asserting—with no evidence whatsoever—that the wall was the sole manmade structure that could be seen from the moon. Some even said that the structure could be glimpsed from Mars. Without question, China's mammoth northern barrier was "the mightiest work of man," proclaimed Robert Ripley, the creator of America's popular "Believe it or Not!" series.[88] Keenly aware of the West's deep admiration for the wall, Sun Zhongshan (Sun Yat-sen), the founder of the new Chinese Republic, hit on the idea of using the Great Wall to promote Chinese nationalism at the critical moment in Chinese history when the country was trying to adjust to life as a republic after more than 20 centuries of imperial rule.

Describing the wall as the chief among the Middle Kingdom's numerous engineering feats, Sun credited the rampart with nothing less than preserving Chinese civilization. Without the Great Wall, he asserted, the Middle Kingdom and its advanced and rich culture would have been obliterated by nomadic tribesmen as early as the Han dynasty (206 B.C.–A.D. 220). Owing to the invaluable protection afforded by the immense northern fortifications, he continued, "Chinese civilization was able to develop in peace until it was strong enough to assimilate even such conquerors as the Yuan [Mongols] and the Qing [Manchus]."[89] According to Arthur Waldron, Sun had an "instinctive sense of what his country needed, and that, above all, was a modern sense of identity: some blend of cultural, racial, and national sentiments" that could replace loyalty to the Middle Kingdom's age-old imperial system. Over the decades following the collapse of China's final dynasty, Sun and his successors' unofficial adoption of the Great Wall as China's national symbol would gradually begin to "fill some of this need."[90]

MAO ZEDONG AND THE GREAT WALL

The unified Chinese Republic founded by Sun Zhongshan in 1912 would prove short-lived. Within three years of its establishment, China had descended into political chaos as powerful regional warlords fought one another for supremacy. By 1930, the militaristic Nationalist Party led by Jiang Jieshi (Chiang Kaishek) had managed to crush the warlords and reunify China but was embroiled in an increasingly violent struggle with the

Communist Party of Mao Zedong. Hostilities between the two rival groups came to a halt during the Sino-Japanese War of 1937–1945 when Japan invaded and occupied northern China but resumed with a vengeance immediately after Japan's defeat.

MAO ZEDONG CELEBRATES THE GREAT WALL IN POEM

Mao Zedong was a poet as well as a political and military leader. In his most famous poem, "Snow," written in 1936, Mao makes the Great Wall a symbol of China's grandeur and compares himself to two of its chief builders and the Middle Kingdom's most forceful rulers, Qin Shi Huang Di and the Han emperor, Wu Di:

This is the scene in that northern land;
A hundred leagues are sealed in ice,
A thousand leagues of whirling snow.
On either side of the Great Wall
One vastness is all you see.
From end to end of the great river
The rushing torrent is frozen and lost.
The mountains dance like silver snakes,
The highlands roll like waxen elephants,
As if they sought to vie with heaven in their height.
And on a sunny day
You will see a red dress thrown over the white,
Enchantingly lovely!
Such great beauty like this in all our landscape
Has caused unnumbered heroes to bow in homage.
But, alas, these heroes—Qin Shi Huang Di and
Han Wu Di . . .
Now they are all past and gone;
To find men truly great and noble-hearted
We must look here in the present.*

*Excerpted from Jonathan Fryer, *The Great Wall of China*, (New York: A.S. Barnes, 1975), p. 186.)

Four years later, in 1949, Mao Zedong and his Red Army finally triumphed over their Nationalist foes. That October, assuring his listeners that the bloodshed, disunity, and humiliation that had beset China for so long were over at last, Mao proclaimed the creation of the Communist People's Republic of China (PRC) from the balcony of Beijing's Gate of Heavenly Peace.

During his long struggles against the Nationalist Party and the Japanese, Mao Zedong had often used the Great Wall as a symbol for China's proud and determined masses. After taking power in 1949, he adopted as the PRC's official anthem a song dating from the Sino-Japanese War. The song, which linked the old defense line with patriotic resistance to Japan, called on all Chinese "who will not be slaves/to take our own flesh and blood, to build a new Great Wall!"[91] Three years later, Mao launched a campaign to renovate several of the most badly eroded sections of the Ming wall near his capital city at Beijing. Nonetheless, during the early decades of the PRC's existence, "the Wall was not yet on center stage."[92] For one thing, few foreign tourists were able to visit the structure because permission to enter the PRC was virtually impossible to obtain. (Nor did many Chinese visit the Wall; the vast majority lacked both the leisure time and the income to travel for pleasure during Mao's 27 years in power.) For another, some Communist hardliners considered the wall an unsuitable emblem for their nation's new proletariat (workers) state. After all, they pointed out, in traditional folk legends like the story of the grieving "wall widow" Meng Jiangnu, the Great Wall had represented the tyranny of the old imperial regime and the cruelty of its oppressive forced labor system.

For a brief time during the political crusade known as the Cultural Revolution (1966–1969), Mao himself turned on the Great Wall. The Cultural Revolution, Mao hoped, would imbue China's youth with the revolutionary fervor he was convinced their elders had lost during the two decades since he had founded the PRC. As part of his new "revolution," Mao urged China's young people to wage war on all remnants of their

During President Nixon's historic 1972 trip to China, Chinese officials brought the president on a tour of the Great Wall. Though China, under the Communist leadership of Mao Zedong, had turned on the Great Wall as a symbol of its pre-Communist past, by the 1970s the Wall had regained its status as a national symbol.

country's pre-communist past. Goaded on by Mao, squads of adolescent Red Guards fanned out through the countryside demolishing anything related to China's traditional culture from ancient Buddhist temples and statues to rare Confucian texts. Nor did the Great Wall escape the Red Guards' wrath. Hundreds of miles of wall were vandalized by Mao's adolescent storm troopers, and huge quantities of stones and bricks were hauled away to use in building roads, dams, houses, and even pigsties.

Three years after inaugurating the Cultural Revolution, even Mao was forced to admit that his campaign to revitalize the PRC's faltering revolutionary spirit had gone too far. Thousands of alleged Chinese "counterrevolutionaries" had been maimed or murdered by his fanatical Red Guards, and countless schools and factories across the nation shut down in the wake of the ever-growing violence and vandalism. With the disbanding of the Red Guards and the end of the Cultural Revolution in 1969, the Great Wall slowly started to regain its former status as a national symbol. In 1972, Richard Nixon made his groundbreaking trip to the People's Republic of China after more than three decades of bitter rivalry between the PRC and the United States. Top-ranking Chinese officials conducted the American president on a highly publicized tour of the Great Wall at Badaling, in the hills northwest of Beijing. "I think that you would have to conclude that this is a great wall and it had to be built by a great people," Nixon proclaimed in a historic speech that signified the beginning of a new era in U.S.-Chinese relations.[93]

"LET US LOVE OUR CHINA AND RESTORE OUT GREAT WALL!"

During the decades since Mao Zedong's death in 1976, the Great Wall has acquired new significance for the Chinese government, economy, and people. Under the leadership of the reform-minded Deng Xiaoping, during the early 1980s, the communist regime committed itself to modernizing the People's Republic, revitalizing its ailing economy and forging closer political, cultural, and commercial ties with the international community. Concerned with bolstering national unity and morale at a time of rapid change in the PRC, Deng Xiaoping and other PRC leaders placed unprecedented emphasis on China's extraordinary cultural heritage. As the government increasingly associated Chinese national pride and identity with the numerous achievements of the country's long civilization, the Great Wall became something to be venerated and protected as a national treasure of virtually unequaled value.

In 1984, Deng Xiaoping launched a highly publicized crusade in China that explicitly tied patriotism to saving and repairing the Great Wall. "Let us love our country and restore our Great Wall," was the campaign's stirring motto.[94] Nature—in the form of rain, snow, wind, and desert sandstorms—had taken an even more terrible toll on the structure than the vandalizing Red Guards, especially in the wall's westernmost section where its earthen sides had never been encased in brick or stone. Now the Chinese government was calling on its people to help preserve and rebuild what remained of the Great Wall's crumbling ramparts and towers.

The task of renovating the wall, which snakes some 2,000 miles (or longer, if all of its various branches are included) through the Chinese countryside has proven a daunting one. To date, most of the restoration work has been carried out at damaged sites close to Beijing, primarily at Badaling (where President Richard Nixon took his historic walk along the wall in 1972) and at Mutianyu, in the low mountains just to the northeast of the capital city. To the dismay of many native and foreign preservationists alike, however, the Chinese government did not stop at repairing the damaged sections of the wall at Badaling and Mutianyu. Eager to promote China's commercial development and especially its burgeoning tourist industry, over the past two decades, the government has allowed the sites to be turned into garish popular attractions. The ancient landmark was soon transformed by cable cars for reaching the wall's crest and toboggans for getting back down the steep hillside, souvenir stands, camel rides, bungee jumping, and American-style fast-food restaurants.

Even in less accessible areas of the structure outside of the capital region, the Great Wall has become a major destination for foreign and Chinese sightseers alike. Many once pristine stretches of the wall now resemble carnivals as much as historic sites, with vendors hawking Great Wall T-shirts, postcards, and other memorabilia; huge billboards promote nearby attractions like water parks, bumper cars, or rifle ranges. At Shanhaiguan, the eastern terminus of the Ming wall, the structure was so eroded that developers essentially fashioned a brand new wall of shiny pewter-colored bricks. They later added a gigantic brick maze for those visitors who did not find exploring the fortifications themselves sufficiently entertaining. In the rampart's remote western stretches, enterprising villagers have set up unauthorized tollbooths and ladders and now charge admission to hikers traversing their community's small piece of the Great Wall.

Today, the Great Wall of China is a symbol of Chinese pride and the achievements of China's ancient civilization. It is considered a national treasure, and millions of tourists visit it every year.

Today, some 10 million foreigners visit China each year; surveys indicate that the vast majority of them make the Great Wall part of their travel itinerary. Even greater numbers of Chinese tour their country's old northern defense line each year, owing in large measure to a recent governmental campaign to boost domestic tourist revenues by implementing a shorter workweek and several new week-long holidays. The wear and tear on the wall from these tourist hordes deeply concerns many conservationists, scholars, and wall enthusiasts. Various preservationist groups, including the China Great Wall Society and the International Friends of the Great Wall, have sponsored clean-up campaigns to remove graffiti and litter. In 2002, the New York-based World Monuments Fund added the Great Wall to its roster of the globe's 100 most endangered sites.

After years of effort, in 2003, preservationists finally secured the first governmental regulation to protect the wall from the onslaught of visitors and the rampant commercial development that has gone hand in hand with China's tourist boom. The new measure creates a 550-yard no-development zone along both sides of the wall and prohibits hiking on the structure except in certain designated tourist areas such as the heavily visited sites at Badaling and Mutianyu. The new ordinance has one major shortcoming: it applies only to the approximately 390 miles of the wall within the municipality of Beijing. As of late 2003, China's central government was still considering regulations that would safeguard the entire wall. Selling the measures to the Chinese public may prove difficult. As the wall's symbolic significance has grown, so, too, has its importance as a moneymaker. It is "asking a lot of Chinese officials to achieve a sophisticated, delicate balance between preservation and tourism in an economically overburdened, developing country," observed one American journalist recently.[95]

The Great Wall's significance for the Chinese people and their leadership has changed enormously over the course of the more than 2,000 years since construction on the barrier began. Like the wall's creator, Qin Shi Huang Di, many of the Middle Kingdom's leaders—including even some of its non-Chinese rulers—placed great faith in the fortifications' ability to safeguard the empire's rich agricultural fields and cities against northern invaders from the steppe. Other dynasties, such as the powerful and cosmopolitan Tang, scorned the huge defensive system as a waste of money and manpower. The wall's importance as a political border as well as a defense line also underwent numerous transformations over the millennia. During the course of the Chinese Empire's long history, the wall was repeatedly repositioned to reflect changing notions of where China should stop and the realm of the Inner Asian nomad should start. Even long after the Great Wall had completely lost its purpose as a military barricade or a national boundary, its significance for the Chinese has continued to develop as a proud symbol of their ancient civilization and as the People's Republic of China most popular—and lucrative—tourist attraction. For its many admirers around the globe, the significance of the arbitrary line of earth and stone first drawn by Qin Shi Huang Di more than two millennia ago to separate the fertile Chinese heartland from the Inner Asian wilderness is perhaps something even greater: a testimony to humankind's ingenuity and will.

circa 700–600 B.C.	First Inter-Kingdom Walls in China are built.
circa 500 B.C.	"True Nomadism" begins in Inner Asia.
403–221 B.C.	During the Warring States Period, northern border walls were built by the kingdoms of Yan, Zhao, and Qin.
221–206 B.C.	The Qin dynasty unites China, and the first Great Wall of Qin Shi Huang Di is erected.
206–202 B.C.–A.D. 220	The Han dynasty extends the Great Wall toward Central Asia.
220–589	Known as the Period of Disunity, this era was marked by intertribal warfare.
386–535	The Northern Wei dynasty extends the Great Wall.
550–577	The Northern Qi dynasty extends the Great Wall.
581–618	Under the Sui dynasty, China is reunited; the Great Wall is extended.
618–907	Under the rule of the Tang dynasty, defensive wall building is scorned.

c. 700–600 B.C.
First Inter-Kingdom Walls in China are erected

221–206 B.C.
The Qin Dynasty unites China; the First Great Wall of Qin Shi Huang Di is erected

220–589
During the Period of Disunity, the Great Wall is extended by the Northern Wei and Qi dynasties

c. 700–600 B.C.   **220–589**

403–221 B.C.
During the Warring States Period, Northern border walls are built by the kingdoms of Yan, Zhao, and Qin

206–202 B.C.–220 A.D.
Under the Han dynasty, the Great Wall is extended toward Central Asia

960–1279	The Song dynasty rules; the Jin empire in the North extends the Great Wall.
1279–1368	The Yuan dynasty (Mongols) rule China.
1368–1644	The Great Wall of the Ming dynasty is constructed; it is to be the greatest and last period of Chinese wall building.
1644–1912	The Qing dynasty (Manchus) rules China until the empire is overthrown.
1912–1949	The Republic of China is established and remains in power until overthrown by communists.
1949–present	The communist government of People's Republic of China rules the country.
1966–1969	The era is marked by the Cultural Revolution of Mao Zedong; parts of the Great Wall are destroyed.
1984	Deng Xiaoping calls for restoration of the Great Wall.
2002	The Great Wall is added to the World Monuments Fund's list of 100 Most Endangered Sites.

581–618
Under the Sui dynasty, China is reunited; the Great Wall is extended

1966–1969
The era is marked by the Cultural Revolution of Mao Zedong; parts of the Great Wall are destroyed

581–618

1984

1279–1368
The Yuan dynasty (Mongols) rule China

1368–1644
The Ming dynasty Great Wall is constructed during the greatest and last period of the Chinese wall building

1984
Deng Xiaoping calls for restoration of the Great Wall

THE PINYIN AND WADE GILES SYSTEMS FOR SPELLING
CHINESE WORDS IN BRITISH

Alphabetic characters are not used in Chinese writing. Consequently, over the centuries several systems for spelling Chinese words and names using the Roman alphabet were developed. Until 1979, when the People's Republic of China adopted the Pinyin system, the most common of these systems was the Wade-Giles. This book uses the Pinyin system for spelling Chinese words in British. However, because readers researching the Great Wall will almost certainly encounter older texts—and even some recent ones—that use the Wade-Giles system, the following chart gives both the Pinyin and Wade-Giles forms for many of the place and personal names mentioned in this volume.

WADE-GILES	PINYIN
Chao	Zhao (ancient state)
Ch'i	Qi (ancient state)
Chin	Jin (dynasty)
Ch'in	Qin (ancient state and dynasty)
Ch'ing	Qing (dynasty)
Ch'inghai	Qinghai (modern-day Chinese province)
Hopei or Hopeh	Hebei (modern-day Chinese province)
Hsien Pei	Xian Bei (a nomadic steppe people)
Hsiung-nu	Xiongnu (a nomadic steppe people)
Kansu	Gansu (modern-day Chinese province)
Liu Pang	Liu Bang (founder of the Han dynasty)
Mao Tse-tung	Mao Zedong (Communist leader of PRC)
Peking	Beijing (capital city of the PRC)
Shansi	Shanxi (modern-day Chinese province)
Shensi	Shaanxi (modern-day Chinese province)
Sinkiang	Xinjiang (modern-day Chinese region)
Ssu-ma Ch'ien	Sima Qian (historian of the Han era)
Sung	Song (dynasty)
T'ai-tsung	Taizong (emperor of the Tang dynasty)
Wu Ti	Wu Di (emperor of the Han dynasty)
Yang Ti	Yang Di (emperor of Sui dynasty)
Zhang Qian	Chang Ch'ien (Han era explorer)

Chapter 1: China's Legendary Northern Wall

1. Andrew J. Nathan and Robert S. Ross, *The Great Wall and the Empty Fortress: China's Search for Security.* New York: W.W. Norton, 1997, p. 24.

Chapter 2: Before the Great Wall

2. Peter Lum, *The Purple Barrier: The Story of the Great Wall of China.* London: Robert Hale, 1960, p. 16.
3. Jonathan Fryer, *The Great Wall of China.* New York: A.S. Barnes, 1975, p. 20.
4. Ibid., p. 20.
5. Quoted in Ibid., p. 62.
6. Ibid., p. 24.
7. Nicola Di Cosmo, *Ancient China and its Enemies: The Rise of Nomadic Power in East Asian History.* Cambridge: Cambridge University Press, 2002, p. 144.
8. Ibid., p. 144.
9. Arthur Waldron, *The Great Wall of China: From History to Myth.* Cambridge: Cambridge University Press, 1990, p. 31.
10. Patricia Buckley Ebrey, *The Cambridge Illustrated History of China.* Cambridge: Cambridge University Press, 1996, p. 164.
11. Di Cosmo, *Ancient China and Its Enemies,* p. 127.
12. Ibid., p. 143.
13. Ibid., p. 149.
14. Ibid., p. 152.
15. Ibid., p. 157.
16. Quoted in Valerie Hansen, *The Open Empire: A History of China to 1600.* New York: W.W. Norton, 2000, pp. 65–66.

Chapter 3: China's First Great Wall: The Wall of Qin Shi Huang Di

17. Ebrey, *Cambridge Illustrated History of China,* p. 63.
18. Quoted in Luo Zewen, Dai Wenbao, Dick Wilson, J. P. Drege, and H. Delahaye, *The Great Wall.* New York: McGraw-Hill, 1981, p. 23.
19. Sima Qian, *Historical Records,* trans. Raymond Dawson. New York: Oxford University Press, 1994, p. 56.
20. Ibid., p. 55.
21. Waldron, *The Great Wall of China,* p. 63.

22. Williamson Murray, MacGregor Knox, and Alvin Bernstein, eds. *The Making of Strategy: Rulers, States, and War.* New York: Cambridge University Press, 1994, p. 105.
23. Sima Qian, *Historical Records,* p. 75.
24. Waldron, *The Great Wall of China,* p. 42–43.
25. Fryer, *The Great Wall of China,* p. 49.
26. Ibid., p. 49.
27. Sima Qian, *Historical Records,* p. 74.
28. Lum, *The Purple Barrier,* p. 57.
29. Hansen, *The Open Empire,* p. 112.
30. Di Cosmo, *Ancient China and Its Enemies,* p. 158.

Chapter 4: The Great Wall of the Han Dynasty

31. Quoted in W. Scott Morton, *China: Its History and Culture.* New York: McGraw-Hill, 1995, p. 50.
32. Waldron, *The Great Wall of China,* p. 34.
33. Sechin Jagchid and Van Jay Symons, *Peace, War, and Trade Along the Great Wall.* Bloomington: Indiana University Press, 1989, p. 23.
34. Quoted in Fryer, *The Great Wall of China,* p. 81.
35. Quoted in Di Cosmo, *Ancient China and its Enemies,* p. 275.
36. Ibid., p. 272.
37. Quoted in Jagchid and Symons, *Peace, War, and Trade Along the Great Wall,* pp. 2–3.
38. Quoted in Di Cosmo, *Ancient China and Its Enemies,* p. 278.
39. Quoted in Waldron, *The Great Wall of China,* p. 41.
40. Di Cosmo, *Ancient China and Its Enemies,* p. 235.
41. Ebry, *Cambridge Illustrated History of China,* p. 69.
42. Fryer, *The Great Wall of China,* p. 82.
43. Morton, *China: Its History and Culture,* p. 56.
44. Ibid., p. 57.

Chapter 5: From the Period of Disunity Through the Mongol Conquest: The Great Wall in War and Peace

45. Ebrey, *Cambridge Illustrated History of China,* p. 92.

46. Waldron, *The Great Wall of China*, p. 44.
47. Ibid., p. 44.
48. Quoted in Ibid., p. 44.
49. Quoted in Ibid., p. 45.
50. Fryer, *The Great Wall of China*, p. 117.
51. Ebrey, *Cambridge Illustrated History of China*, p. 111.
52. Ibid., p. 111.
53. Quoted in Luo Zewen et. al., *The Great Wall*, p. 42.
54. John Minford and Joseph S. M. Lau, eds., *Classical Chinese Literature: An Anthology of Translations*. New York: Columbia University Press, 2000, Vol. I, p. 831.
55. Ebrey, *Cambridge Illustrated History of China*, p. 169.
56. William Lindesay, *The Great Wall: The Genius of China*. Hong Kong: The Guidebook Company, 1998, p. 14.
57. J.A.G. Roberts, *A Concise History of China*. Cambridge: Harvard University Press, 1999, p. 104.
58. Fryer, *The Great Wall of China*, p. 135.
59. Waldron, *The Great Wall of China*, p. 51.
60. Ebrey, *Cambridge Illustrated History of China*, p. 173.
61. Ibid., p. 182.

Chapter 6: The Ming Wall

62. Quoted in Ann Paludan, *Chronicle of the Chinese Emperors: The Reign-by-Reign Record of the Rulers of Imperial China*. London: Thames and Hudson, 1998, p. 161.
63. Fryer, *The Great Wall of China*, p. 139.
64. Hansen, *The Open Empire*, p. 377.
65. Paludan, *Chronicle of the Chinese Emperors*, p. 166.
66. Quoted in Murray, Knox, and Bernstein, eds., *The Making of Strategy*, p. 104.
67. Waldron, *The Great Wall of China*, p. 88.
68. Quoted in Hansen, *The Open Empire*, p. 385.
69. Waldron, *The Great Wall of China*, p. 127; Michael D. Swaine and Ashley J. Tellis, *Interpreting China's Grand Strategy: Past, Present, and Future* (Rand, 3 March 2004), http://rand.org/publications/MR/MR1121
70. Quoted in Ibid., p. 127.
71. Quoted in Ibid., p. 41.
72. Fryer, *The Great Wall of China*, p. 145.
73. Waldron, *The Great Wall of China*, p. 110.
74. Quoted in Jagchid and Symons, *Peace, War, and Trade Along the Great Wall*, p. 3.
75. Murray, Knox, and Bernstein, eds., *The Making of Strategy*, p. 100.
76. Waldron, *The Great Wall of China*, p. 141.
77. Lindesay, *The Great Wall*, p. 25.

Chapter 7: The Great Wall in Western and Chinese Eyes

78. F. W. Mote, *Imperial China, 900–1800* (Cambridge: Harvard University Press, 1999), p. 696.
79. Quoted in Waldron, *The Great Wall of China*, p. 206.
80. Quoted in Robert Silverberg, *The Long Rampart: The Story of the Great Wall of China*. Philadelphia: Chilton Books, 1966, p. 143.
81. Quoted in Fryer, *The Great Wall of China*, p. 173.
82. Quoted in Ibid., p. 173.
83. Quoted in Waldron, *The Great Wall of China*, p. 208.
84. Quoted in Ibid., p. 209.
85. Quoted in Luo Zewen et. al., *The Great Wall*, p. 178.
86. Quoted in Ibid., p. 179.
87. Quoted in Ibid., p. 179.
88. Quoted in Waldron, *The Great Wall of China*, p. 214.
89. Ibid., p. 215.
90. Ibid., p. 215.
91. Quoted in Ibid., p. 216.
92. Ibid., p. 217.
93. Quoted in Fryer, *The Great Wall of China*, p. 188.
94. Quoted in Waldron, *The Great Wall of China*, p. 221.
95. Michael A. Lev, "China's Hiking Ban Aims to Save Great Asset," *Chicago Tribune*, September 12, 2003.

Di Cosmo, Nicola. *Ancient China and Its Enemies: The Rise of Nomadic Power in East Asian History.* Cambridge: Cambridge University Press, 2002.

Ebrey, Patricia Buckley. *The Cambridge Illustrated History of China.* Cambridge: Cambridge University Press, 1996.

Fryer, Jonathan. *The Great Wall of China.* New York: A. S. Barnes, 1975.

Hansen, Valerie. *The Open Empire: A History of China to 1600.* New York: W. W. Norton, 2000.

Hesler, Peter. "Chasing the Wall," *National Geographic,* January 2003, pp. 2–33.

Jagchid, Sechin, and Van Jay Symons. *Peace, War, and Trade Along the Great Wall.* Bloomington: Indiana University Press, 1989.

Lev, Michael A. "China's Hiking Ban Aims to Save Great Asset," *Chicago Tribune,* September 12, 2003.

Lindesay, William. *The Great Wall: The Genius of China.* Hong Kong: The Guidebook Company, 1998.

Liu, Melinda. "The Late Great Wall," *Newsweek,* July 29, 2002, pp. 40–43.

Lum, Peter. *The Purple Barrier: The Story of the Great Wall of China.* London: Robert Hale, 1960.

Luo Zewen, Dai Wenbao, Dick Wilson, J.P. Drege, and H. Delahaye. *The Great Wall,* New York: McGraw-Hill, 1981.

Minford, John, and Joseph S. M. Lau, eds. *Classical Chinese Literature: An Anthology of Translations.* New York: Columbia University Press, 2000, Vol. I.

Morton, W. Scott. *China: Its History and Culture.* New York: McGraw-Hill, 1995.

Mote, F.W. *Imperial China, 900–1800.* Cambridge: Harvard University Press, 1999.

Murray, Williamson, MacGregor Knox, and Alvin Bernstein, eds. *The*

Making of Strategy: Rulers, States, and War. New York: Cambridge University Press, 1994.

Nathan, Andrew J., and Robert S. Ross. *The Great Wall and the Empty Fortress: China's Search for Security.* New York: W. W. Norton, 1997.

Paludan, Ann. *Chronicle of the Chinese Emperors: The Reign-by-Reign Record of the Rulers of Imperial China.* London: Thames and Hudson, 1998.

Roberts, J.A.G. *A Concise History of China.* Cambridge: Harvard University Press, 1999.

Schwartz, Daniel. *The Great Wall of China.* London: Thames & Hudson, 2001.

Silverberg, Robert. *The Long Rampart: The Story of the Great Wall of China.* Philadelphia: Chilton Books, 1966.

Sima Qian. *Historical Records.* trans. Raymond Dawson. New York: Oxford University Press, 1994.

Swaine, Michael D. and Ashley J. Tellis. "Interpreting China's Grand Strategy: Past, Present, and Future." Rand, 3 March 2004, http://rand.org/publications/MR/MR1121

Waldron, Arthur. *The Great Wall of China: From History to Myth.* Cambridge: Cambridge University Press, 1990.

Du Temple, Lesley A. *The Great Wall of China*. Minneapolis, MN: Lerner, 2003.

McNeese, Tim. *The Great Wall of China*. San Diego: Lucent, 1997.

Silverberg, Robert. The Long Rampart: The Story of the Great Wall of China. Philadelphia: Chilton Books, 1966.

WEBSITES

CHINA: THE GREAT WALL
www.geocities.com/greatwallofChina2000

THE GREAT WALL
www.travelchinaguide.com/China_great_wall/index.html

THE GREAT WALL: A VIRTUAL TOUR
www.chinavista.com/travel/greatwall/greatwall.html

nomadic groups driven out by, 42
peace treaty with, 43–5
threat from, 39, 41–2

Yan, kingdom of, 11, 12, 16–8
Yang Di, 60–1
Yangzi River, 61
Yanjing (Jurchen capital), 68
Yellow River, 27–8, 61

Yong Le, 74–5, 78–9
Yuan dynasty, 70–1
Yuezhi tribe, 49

Zhang Juzheng, 81–2
Zhao, kingdom of, 11, 12, 16–8, 20
Zheng, (king) ("Tiger of Qin"), 21
Zhengtong (Ming emperor), 77–8
Zhongguo (Middle Kingdom), 21

page:

Frontis: 21st Century Publishing
3   New Millennium Images
9   New Millennium Images
24 New Millennium Images
31 New Millennium Images
35 KRT/NMI
52 21st Century Publishing

62 New Millennium Images
67 New Millennium Images
76 New Millennium Images
82 New Millennium Images
98 AP/Wide World Photos
101 New Millennium Images

Louise Chipley Slavicek received her master's degree in history from the University of Connecticut. She has written many articles on historical topics for young people's magazines and is the author of nine other books for young people, including Women of the American Revolution, Israel, Abraham Lincoln, and Mao Zedong. She lives in Ohio with her husband Jim, a research biologist, and their two children, Krista and Nathan.

George J. Mitchell served as chairman of the peace negotiations in Northern Ireland during the 1990s. Under his leadership, an historic accord, ending decades of conflict, was agreed to by the governments of Ireland and the United Kingdom and the political parties in Northern Ireland. In May 1998, the agreement was overwhelmingly endorsed by a referendum of the voters of Ireland, North and South. Senator Mitchell's leadership earned him worldwide praise and a Nobel Peace Prize nomination. He accepted his appointment to the U.S. Senate in 1980. After leaving the Senate, Senator Mitchell joined the Washington, D.C. law firm of Piper Rudnick, where he now practices law. Senator Mitchell's life and career have embodied a deep commitment to public service and he continues to be active in worldwide peace and disarmament efforts.

James I. Matray is professor of history and chair at California State University, Chico. He has published more than forty articles and book chapters on U.S.-Korean relations during and after World War II. Author of *The Reluctant Crusade: American Foreign Policy in Korea, 1941–1950* and *Japan's Emergence as a Global Power,* his most recent publication is *East Asia and the United States: An Encyclopledia of Relations Since 1784.* Matray also is international columnist for the *Donga Ilbo* in South Korea.